A HEALER'S JOURNEY WITH ELEMENTALS, SPIRIT AND PURPOSE

by
Sue Oosterwoud

Blessings
Sve
Oosterw

MAPLE
PUBLISHERS

E S P (A Healer's Journey with Elementals, Spirit and Purpose)

Author: Sue Oosterwoud

Copyright © 2024 Sue Oosterwoud

The right of Sue Oosterwoud to be identified as author of this work has been asserted by the author in accordance with section 77 and 78 of the Copyright, Designs and Patents Act 1988.

ISBN 978-1-83538-186-1 (Paperback)
        978-1-83538-187-8 (E-Book)

Cover Design and Book Layout by:
        White Magic Studios
        www.whitemagicstudios.co.uk

Published by:
        Maple Publishers
        Fairbourne Drive, Atterbury,
        Milton Keynes,
        MK10 9RG, UK
        www.maplepublishers.com

This book is dedicated to Taeke, my soul mate who now works to the rhythms of ethereal harmonies, and ever holds my hand and guides me onwards.

United we live For Life And Love for Eternity

Contents

Chapter 1

Meeting the Past

The pain in my left forearm was searing hot. I could feel my systems within, alert yet calm, sensing out the source. Wisps of smoke wafted ethereally through the hallway window. Sheer blistering burning agony, it ramped up to another level of pain as I stepped through the lounge door, moving closer to the source.

A woman's desperate cries were audible from the corner of the room and the stench of choking smoke was obvious. The lounge however was physically ship shape and neat... A surreal setting to view the smoke, the burning and the anguished cries amidst.

I was aware of the homeowner staring at me with frightened eyes from the hall. "Is smoke one of the phenomena you have been experiencing?" I asked. I needed to make this quick, the burn was bloody killing even though no physical sign of it was there. She nodded, then began to try to tell me more. "No," my interjection was a bit sharp but there was no time to waste. "We'd rather tell you what we find. Please go outside and play with your son in the garden while I attend to some work in here." She could sense it well enough, she scuttled off at high speed.

The door firmly closed behind me, I turned and re-tuned into the scene. It had become even more intense and audible and physically distressing. I would be on my own for another good 30 minutes yet but I had no choice, I would just have to go it alone. Breathing deeply to slow and calm my systems. I closed my eyes and focused. The first seconds of travelling visually through the 3rd eye is a glorious sense that beckons you to just zip off on some awesome trip, however the need and the intensity of this was not going to allow any 'space tourism' today. Almost immediately the lounge disappeared and the ground opened up beneath my feet. I was falling deeper and deeper and the further I fell, the longer this took, would determine just how far back in history the answers lay.

Minutes passed and then everything turned red, searing molten red. The cries from the woman stood out, even amidst the acrid smoke, the burning devastation and the palpable fear all around.

"A fine day to meet hell all on one's tod," I thought. The day my sense of humour didn't travel with me would be the day my kit box was a major tool too light.

The poor woman was crouched, one arm protectively clutching a baby, the other reaching out into the flames, desperately trying to grasp and pull another loved one from the fire. Her own terror and desire to save overriding the horrendous pain I knew too well she was locked in.

Time does not exist. Nor if time did, has it the ability to heal when trauma so deep and immense has scarred a land. And this woman was one of many hundreds. However her suffering was representative of all. Take her away from this hell she was locked in and many more lives would be freed too. This was carnage on a mass scale.

I tore my focus from the woman and projected clearly that I was ready for her lost loved one to come. There she was, just a little girl, 4 or 5 years old, standing surrounded by poppies.

Poppies grow where battles have been fought, where blood has been spilled. My warning, if I didn't already know, that this centuries old fire was no accident.

The little girl though was so happy. Perhaps even in the midst of such a distressing death a child will pass over easier. However a mother's guilt can blind her from being reachable and hold her with the mass of emotion and sheer trauma the others are locked within too. I found myself on my knees simultaneously beckoning the little girl towards her mother whilst breaking through her cries with a strong command, "Stop look to your right. The fire is gone, your child is safe."

If the woman had had form the strength of the command would have shaken her physically. She stopped. Disbelief, relief, a scream of elation. She turned. She ran. The exhilarating pure joy lit her face as she encircled her child – the baby, the mother, the girl a huddle of joyous relief. The atmosphere audibly snapped, lifted, lightened. The mother and her children disappeared as many more lost tortured souls followed her eagerly towards their joyful reunions. As the last of them passed finally over to the peace and solace that held its arms open wide, the heat and noise finally died away. The portal closed, the earth returned beneath me. I was back on the familiar lounge carpet, soaked with sweat, and drained.

As my systems returned, my first awareness was that the burning pain in my left arm was gone. My first task was complete. I disregarded the aching and throbbing in my knees and shins and placed my forehead and palms flat on the floor. "Thank you, thank you, thank you. Rest, be at peace." A mantra of gratitude repeated, the only consciousness present that of the overwhelming sense of appreciation and awe for the loving hands that guide and the miracle of the human systems that travel to this work so clearly.

Just as I began to unfurl and begin the painful process of allowing blood to flow back into my deadened feet and aching limbs, I heard Donna, my therapy partner, rush through the door with a hasty apology to the homeowner. "My God, are you ok? The last 30 minutes in the car was hell driving here. I was suffocating with the smoke, I knew you were in it. I've just been trying to send help to you, trying to stay calm, and drive." Her words tailed off, the evidence of much work done was clear from my general rather dishevelled appearance.

So, she helped me up. Let me come round, let me readjust. No words were spoken as she sensed the room, the house, the land it stood on. Finally we looked at each other knowingly. We had been landed another big job. It had happened pretty much from the moment we met; destiny had its plans, and we were taken along with them. Distressed land, houses with curious issues found their way to draw us to them. Often it presented as seemingly a small task, a minor issue. And then like a little paranormal jack in the box out it all popped!

And by then we were in, hook, line and sinker, usually up to our neck in cries for healing we could no way let down. I was just glad she could feel too the deep aching need this house and land were emitting to us.

We nodded in unison, agreeing without words to the knowing that we were committing to a full day of intense work. Donna led the way out into the back garden, up the steps, to the perimeter wall. We both stared out across the rising fields to the horizon.

"They came from there," she said, "a whole army of them. It was centuries ago. They killed the men, burned the settlement to the ground. They didn't stand a chance. It's awful."

I stared, my vision again adjusting to see the rising mass of the army, their imprint clear on the horizon. A rush of forgiveness surged through me. "They want this all to end now too," I said. "Their guilt and shame has kept them here watching the distress they caused to the land and those people. They want to make it right."

There was no difference in the sadness I felt for the people who had lived here to the men who had perpetrated the harm. Judgment is not present in the realm of healing. Its purity of love is there for all. And the best owed to the land through human deed would first need to be paid. There was an honour in being called to this task. Before we could begin to communicate with the land further, to find the ways it held to bring closure and peace for it, we needed to speak with the homeowner. The lady present was due some explanation and needed reassurance too.

I had taken little detail of the disturbances and phenomena that had been occurring, preferring to evidence our work by confirming details. The job had now grown from the perimeters of cleansing a house to an entire landmass spanning some miles. She needed to know that the extra healing work we would be doing before we could resume our focus on the house would cost her no more. Thankfully she was very open minded, but then most people were when they had been experiencing visual and audible disturbances there was no 'usual' way to explain away.

It was a beautiful clear sunny day, perfect for working outdoors, so we gathered on the patio and explained what had happened. The 'smoke' had regularly been wafting through the hallway window and there were numerous more curious appearances that had been witnessed and also recorded by cameras they had positioned around the house.

We stifled any attempts at describing these and said that the cameras would need switching off later. Unfortunately these, in an 'active' environment, had a tendency to attract all sorts of energetic 'life' in to 'perform' a turn and it was generally the more strange, mischievous and noisy realms that rather enjoyed creating their own dramas the theatre of appearance cameras and filming provided! It often made things a little too busy to get to the cause and need when 'extras' were wandering in and out too!

"When did all this begin to kick off?" I enquired, knowing the family was not new to the house. "Everything was fine," the lady replied, "until we dug up the drive and then wham stuff just started to happen. What have we done wrong?" it was starting to make sense why the strongest appearance had come from the lounge first which was positioned at the front with the new drive running directly before and up to the window where the woman had appeared.

Placing my hand on hers I began to reassure her that actually their actions were providing a great service, so often digging, building, restorations, small and major changes disturbed, or allowed, trauma or energetic prints to surface. The 'memory' of this trauma had been buried deep in the ground and digging and excavating had simply allowed the land to reveal it. "We will be shown what is the correct way to heal this fully," I assured her.

She looked down at my hand still resting on hers. "That's why you got the job," she replied smiling. "When you replied to my email you said you were sensing the house as you wrote but had to stop writing as you couldn't feel your ring finger anymore." I nodded quizzically, remembering. "That's when I knew you were a genuine sensitive. My husband has the end of that finger missing."

Donna and I had to apologize for falling about laughing. So often the oddest and smallest registrations, visions and signs were the most imperative of all and we had often learnt the hard way not to ignore them. "God is in the detail," I laughed. "And now we had better get back to work, this land has waited long enough for this day."

Today, over six years on from that day, I have greater understanding that the more huge and vast the healing required is, the more powerful, intense and truly stunning the process. The level of energy, so real, yet magical, the sources that bring this and, do the work of this, will be. To truly proffer the worlds of energy, healing and the Earth, the value and respect that this land and house cleanse heralded that day, it would be wisest to return to this story later. For so much lead us to this point of capability and trust, to find ourselves amidst this and numerous more mysterious and incredible experiences after.

This is a piece of sky in a huge and still beautifully incomplete jigsaw puzzle of life and before we continue with the sky we should piece together more of the ground. It is said a picture paints a thousand words. The pictures on each piece in this puzzle tells a sequential true story of how extraordinary and magical human life can be in harmony with this sacred Earth upon which we place our feet. That mine would be so blessed is still a source of great wonder and joy to me. Far too wonderful to not be shared.

Chapter 2

Finding the Present

"What are we going to do when you grow up?" That 'polite' conversation adults would make. "We'll grow bigger," the little voice of my childhood companion would say. Then we'd disappear together back into our private little world where books fuelled our imagination. We loved Enid Blyton. It would be a long time before I knew who my companion was, for why would I think to ask? My childhood years were accompanied so naturally, my friend just felt a part of me.

Even when, years later, I found myself in a healing session holding the hand of a beautiful little spirit child who was pointing very crossly at the lady lying on the couch, I didn't wonder why my childhood companion had indeed grown bigger with me. "She," cried the indignant little girl, "does not play with me anymore." I was focusing, with difficulty, on inviting in a relative or friend to collect her. The pains in my lower legs were hugely distracting. "I had terrible growing pains," the lady said. "I don't think they were yours," I replied.

Young lives, it seems, need to fully pass over to grow, to move forwards. The memory of play with her "invisible" friend was clear in her. Before the little girl would leave with the children beckoning her over, she needed acknowledging, needed words a child could understand

and that precious moment to be hugged, to dance around her long-loved companion, to gently realize this life had grown up.

As painful as that maturing and separation had been, the physical form must grow, it won't be stunted by another's fear of growth, of walking freely into the next phase of life. We said, "Thank you for the play, for being a friend." Told her, "People grow up and get older here, and can't play so much anymore. But lots of children were waiting over there to run, dance and play." Following our gaze she happily ran to her new-found friends, a little companion that was intended to leave, whilst mine was intended to stay. And one day, a longtime ahead, we would hug too. I would know who my companion is.

Guidance is subtle, you must have a quiet openness inside to hear the hints, the nudges, the clues. You must stay awake to life, learn to surrender and not resist the invisible strings that pull you along. Often we will ask for 'What's next to appear now' and something will happen, manifest in the arena of life, but it won't be what we expected it to be. So, we ignore it, walk away from it, avoid it, only for it to appear again.

The very same learning, same answer, yet in a different way. The further you travel with trust and belief the more you realise how often loving unseen ears have heard and unseen hands have answered with a gifting into your life to help. It's examined, considered, but it's not quite as we anticipated. So we hand the gift back saying we don't like the wrapping. It returns in a different packaging, what's inside has remained the same. It would be remarkably handy if, in teenage years and our twenties, guiding hands and ears could forgo the subtleties.

During those years, big directional signposts with arrows on and angels hammering the answers in with lumps of 4" by 2" planks would really help. Within the confines and permissions guidance has, mine did find a way. After a period of seeming separation when my companion spoke again, the voice had been raised by many decibels. And what had once felt a part of me from within began to come audibly through my right ear. But, not a word was uttered about what I would do when I grew up, and needing some definition had begun to become imminent because physically I was doing just that!

I was 14 and had dithered over the subject choices at school. The stupid boxes were not organized at all how I wanted them to be. It was like a box of chocolates with all the good ones in one section of the box but you could only could pick one, and then a whole ¾ of the rest of the box filled with all the coffee creams. You could have lots of those and I didn't want any of them.

That's the first time I found I was very good at knowing what I did *not* want to do. Finding my own way in what life intended for me was going to be damn slow if it had to be done by a process of elimination. As far as I could see the world had an awful lot of stuff I didn't want.

Working to solely pursue money confused me. Just as Douglas Adam's 'Hitchhikers Guide to the Galaxy' so aptly described the puzzlement in an alien race observing humans all dashing around after little pieces of blue paper – known then as the £5.00 note to earthlings. I really understood those aliens! Vegetarianism was lurking around the corner, more by instinct than knowledge at that time. And 'owning stuff' was equally mysterious, I couldn't fathom with death and all, how that could work at all. Being blessed with a wonderful family, the value and reason for *that* I could get. It wasn't however helping with the choices boxes or making 'career options' any clearer.

It was morning break time and I was heading down the corridor to the stairs when the 'Shorthand Typing' teacher appeared. She was a short, trim, powerful little Scottish woman and I could see by her face that somehow I had royally pissed her off. Accordingly she began to confirm this in a staccato of broad clipped verbal rebukes. This was an unfortunately timed meeting. Most of my brain was focused on the Bounty Bar in my bag. I would need to tear some neurons away from that to decipher her thick accent. I leaned in closer, hoping that would help, which wasn't pleasing as she had memorable bad breath. Luckily she had much to say so I began to get the gist. Girls that were proficient in English chose Shorthand and Typing. As I had scored top in my year in English, just as all girls who had gone before me had done, she had expected that I would *sensibly* choose Shorthand and Typing. But it was not just a coffee cream to me, it was a half chewed by a mangy dog and spat out coffee cream. This was the end of the '70's – the ownership of a pair of boobs and a good command of the English language equalled secretary it seemed.

My knitted brow was not pleasing her, and I was physically recoiling with indignation that this teacher thought she could decide for me that my destiny lay in some stuffy office banging on typewriter keys and putting poor bits of tree into alphabetical order. The relief of being out of range of the dragon's breath of halitosis enabled my remaining neurons to raise themselves from their odour induced coma.

The Bounty bar could wait, the time was now to strike a blow for New Woman. "No. Absolutely No. I cannot, I will not, ever work in an office."

Her mouth formed a shape I had not seen before. The human form was fascinating! But, before I could get sidetracked, my mouth opened and began to speak again. "In fact I am instead going to accounts. Book keeping is useful for running a business."

The birthing of the rebel in me had happened. God bless that teacher for her midwifery!

Boys chose accounts! I had struck out at conformity and found one of my major tools in my life kit box of discerning what I did want to do. There would be much learning ahead to discern when resistance was needed to bring the right kind of struggles. I would often be the proverbial weed that grew through the tarmac, the errant seedling that refused the stiflingly unnatural flower bed row and threw itself to the wind trusting the powers of nature to carry it to its true home.

As I was trying to catch up with myself I realized my reply had been received like a fox in a hen house. She was already fleeing down the corridor, her feathers visibly ruffled. 'Like a Jack Russell,' I thought unwrapping my Bounty bar, 'short legged and snappy.' The joys of tropical island coconut soon enabled the combat to fade, and two years later, for no greater defined reason than a liking for baking, and my best friend extolling the virtues of signing up for catering college where, at not yet 17, we would be able to board all week which sounded fun, I plumped for a 2-year Diploma course and headed off there too.

Now, the arena of what is termed 'Front of House' was a huge source of enjoyment to me.

People fascinated me and the restaurant, bar and reception afforded lots of sociable engagement, interspersed with training your memory to mastermind level and working on developing varicose veins the size of grapes before age 20! There was also a section of the kitchen called the 'Still Room'. Despite its name it is not a small hallowed meditative sanctuary for trainee Buddhist chefs.

Gorgeous aromas of coffee spike your senses to their full alertness creating the speed and intensity needed to meet the demands of perfectly laid silverware pots, jugs and sugar bowls presented on doilyed trays accompanied by delicate cups and saucers for a myriad of suitably attired diners to quaff.

Along with the neat little pockets formed from the paper napkins and constructed for no other reason than to house toast fingers, the over embellishment of simple beverages and origami lessons for toasted bread was an eyebrow raising source of amusement to me.

However frustrating the endeavour of separating doily's was... nigh on impossible to reach a singular sheet without tweezers and a toothpick... and amusing that grown adults needed their pate accompanied by toast soldiers with the crust removed, I very soon found myself yearning to bolt to that caffeine-soaked corner once I discovered the bigger arena it was tucked away from.

The simple art of walking is vastly impaired when clad in kitchen 'whites' that have been starched to levels of stiffness that cause physical pain on movement. I had barely been acquainted with my apron, which had no need of my body to transport it around; it could stand completely independently and was vigorously fighting with my knee joints' choice to bend slightly to walk normally, when I entered the vast monstrous arena of steel that is a catering kitchen. Cloying blast furnace heat which has reached a volcanic level that then requires an extraction unit to kick in, it's in breath causes all voices to rise to above raucous school yard level to communicate 'normally' and anything not secured by straps, bolts or screws takes off on a direct flight path into its jaws.

Gripping my hat, not by fashion choice, but health and hygiene requirements, I viewed ovens the size of giant Fiat Puntos, and steel worktops I had only previously seen the like of on T.V. with dead bodies on. Within 10 minutes I had followed instructions to check on the contents of one oven and failed due to the heat welding my mascara clad eyelashes together. Before the steam had even encouraged the first unimaginable sized spots to emerge on my cheeks, I had filed the kitchen completely and irrevocably in my *do not want* section.

Sunday school had taught me that Hell was hot. Clearly the vicar had also been to catering college before the Good Lord called him to serve. A vow of celibacy did actually appeal more in that moment but thankfully youth allows such madness to disappear quickly.

While I was locked in my inner battle of a future devoid of kitchens and sex, everyone else appeared to have found their joy, revelling in new creativity and steam bathing themselves into some culinary heaven that was clearly totally unreachable from the home planet I orbited on. I was as stiff as a peg doll, with eyelashes that had been flambéed, viewing a scene that was totally beyond me. 'Take a sauna if you love heat this much. Get a package deal and Ambré Solaire yourself to a crisp by the pool.' Why it had to be accompanied by the dismembered limbs of farmyard animals and tomato skins awkwardly rolled into a rose shape I just did not know.

I would later grow great respect and appreciation for chefs and realise, for those who thrive and flourish in that environment, stress and pressure forces their creation to appear, to emerge. And that 'need' and 'addiction' to stress to succeed, to push the extraordinary to happen is at the core of many professions today. Its life span is short, and so too is the persons' tenure who does not develop into other realms and ways to be. For me heat, noise, the compression of stress would only ever close me down. The road to expansive, reflective spaces is longer, more solitary and although more true, kinder and more natural for the full development of the human systems, viewed as odd and often ridiculed. But in a world addicted to speed and fast results even that which is obviously true must be derided lest it challenge a major pivot in the hamster wheel, for the faster it turns the more profit is made.

Entering that kitchen for me was like a 19th century weaver being thrashed to a spinning jenny. I loved to bake a sponge, cut out a few rounds of scones. I could never be a Chef, the love of creating lay for me in process and a speed of production that was clearly imbued in my being from centuries past.

Despite my total dislike of the cooking elements of the course and spending most of the Butchery classes in the First Aid room being bandaged, due to the very sharp boning knives and an aversion to slicing through flesh other than my own, I somehow managed to complete my first year. Amazing, what can be achieved even with much of your upper body in a mummified state!

By the 2nd year of college I was the proud owner of a scooter and began a weekend job in a local restaurant. It was my first night, and it may have been nerves that closed a small distance that teenage years had brought between my faithful childhood friend and me. It may have been the warm and welcoming team of staff who became the closest and most hilarious work friends I ever had. That combination was perhaps inseparable in enabling myself and my companion to share a moment that set a precedent for life ahead.

Having been familiarized with the restaurant I was led into the kitchen where, beyond the hot plates, a melée of steam, heat and activity was in full swing. The waiter beside me pointed to a tall slender blond man who was delivering instructions in a strong foreign accent. "Meet Taeke, the Head Chef," he announced. As he turned towards me, his "Hello" was completely drowned out by a loud voice in my right ear, "That's the man you will marry". Before I could comprehend the words a light show began to fizz and pop in front of my eyes. Bright sparks like fireworks and an intense laser beam of light shot between me and the owner of the outstretched hand in front of me. "He's Dutch," the waiter said, "They shake hands," clearly wondering why mine wasn't ready to meet it.

It was obvious, for them nothing unusual had occurred, they had not seen or heard anything. Yet I felt like I had travelled through some invisible checkpoint. As if I had been travelling a road and had passed through an important marker I had no idea was a destination or a pivotal point. I looked at Taeke. I instantly knew the voice was right. He was a destination, not a passing station on this journey. What friend could know me so well? Know my destiny? Know his destiny? Love me enough to know that something in me would accept and hear and see so clearly?

As stunning, as magical, as important as that moment was, I accepted it naturally, soaked it into my being, aware of the bright flame in me burning ever brighter, but continuing my life, dating, completing college and never speaking to anyone of what I knew.

Two months before my 20th birthday we married, having dated for just nine months. That intense laser beam of connection kept shining with us for the next 33 years. It still binds us despite his call too early to leave this Earth. Another level of communion and guidance together to write the journey of next. Although there would be many times ahead that guiding voice would pick up its loud hailer to deliver its prophetic words, the gradual surrender and melting of resistant heart and mind pathways enables the guidance to become quieter again. It is natural for the instinct and intuition to inhabit an almost magical space of 'knowing' and spin invisible threads that sense our feelings and thoughts acutely. Response develops into an unconscious trust until you and the guidance merge as one again, just as it was as a child.

I was, however, treated to this stunning display of energetic fireworks once again, over 20 years on, from meeting Taeke for the first time. By then our daughter, Saskia, was over 18 years old and the three of us had called into a Bistro for lunch. The Bistro in a 5-storey building, we lovingly converted and ran as a coffee shop, restaurant and wine bar for 10 years. From the age of one Sas had known the building as home as we lived in the rooftop flat above the business. It was strange returning there, 7 years on from leaving, as a customer. We had a close relationship with the building, which held a lot of history, memories and stories to tell within its walls. The universe was about to indelibly print one more happy memory into the fabric of its being and cause me to wonder how such artful, strategic, cosmic planning could ever have been reduced to the word 'coincidence'. It's like labelling a diamond with the word 'Glass'.

Out the kitchen the Head-Chef strode and I could almost smell the sulphur as an invisible sparkler lit. Seconds feel like minutes when that heightened awareness throws you into your instinctive systems and smell, sight and hearing move into an octave that animals inhabit every moment of their lives. I could hear the electrified air crackle as Saskia's eyes met his and wham, there it was again, like cosmic comets on a collision course, the laser beam shot between them leaving the tail of the comet fizzing and popping along the indelible string of connection – wow! Being privy to *that* moment with them and witnessing the awesome power of the mystery of love and connection yet again was like a whole chorus of angels shouting, "Hey, remember this!"

And then allowing me to witness two of the most precious people feel Cupid's arrow magically pull them together. Although the light show was out of the range of others' eyes they were both of course swept up in its orbit and destiny repeated itself by creating a perfect match. Love has an intensity, power and a mission all of its own. Being swept into the role of observer, to view from the outside, the delights of the inevitable happening is also a sweet and generous reminder of life's precious moments.

So, when I looked into the eyes of our first grandchild just 16 months later, I was transported right back to the moment at birth when Saskia first fixed me in her gaze. The midwife who delivered Saskia had a positively angelic glow. I have met and seen this pure energy in nurses and those in caring roles since, and what attends, works through and with those lives is stunning beyond words. There is something deeply sacred, revered and held in very high esteem by higher realms for that active life within certain people, which compels them to bring relief to others.

The universe orders its importance, and thus its value system, in a far more true and logical way than it has yet been able to manifest widely on Earth's 'social structure'. However, beyond the confines of that culture, within each of us, we intuitively know that the richest and most valuable parts of life are the same memorable moments for all, whether famous, rich or otherwise and those who touch our hearts will be the same simple folk we know ourselves to be. The hands that guide a baby from the mysterious world of the womb to its first moments on earth are very special indeed.

As captivated as I was by the midwife's radiant aura, she equally seemed captivated by Saskia and when she handed her to me I realised why. The intensity of her gaze totally transfixed me and a rush of questions coursed through me. If a bugle had sounded in my right ear I could not have been more aware that I was about to be spoken to. "This child has come to teach you." The voice held no sense of warning, the message was simply and clearly a kindly way of letting me know that life so far had been taxiing down the runway and the heights ahead would be peppered with 'air traffic control' instructions. Saying a silent prayer that Saskia's first teaching would be how terry nappies and pins combined to create successful waterproof attire, I mentally buckled my seat belt and stowed away the lap tray.

It was now blatantly clear that a mere trickle of words had so far held an ocean of truth. 'Life is about to get very busy' I thought. "No shit, Sherlock. There's no time for an inflight movie and peanuts either." My brain seemed to have developed a life of its own, but it appears that at the point of take-off I acquired an extra passenger with a big sense of humour. That extra source of wisdom interspersed with regular bouts of hilarity was going to prove vital ahead. And yet again the words just seemed to soak naturally into my being and awaken signals in my inner lives. It was as if these moments were codes that switched lights on to be ready ahead.

There was a growing awareness that others did not share this same familiarity with guiding hands and words but it felt so normal to me to know completely that human life is loved and accompanied. To not trust, to question too deeply, such care and kindness would dishonour a loyalty that was due the same return. That my brain seemed to now have its own communication network hooked up to a part of the universe reserved for comic one liners proved that what you needed on life's journey would be issued at the point it was required! I would discover later what this bright mischievous network actually is and why its nature is different to the other guiding source. As our new little life began to grow, so too did a deep sense of awe in the profound mystery of human appearance, life, Earth, the universe and more.

Accompanying that came a huge sense of responsibility about bringing a life into this world, about care taking her life to be as her destiny intended. A deeper respect and gratitude for Earth, for the potential life holds to play a part in creating change, led me to actively campaign for environmental and humanitarian issues. The more I read and understood about resources and pollution the more I realised of the intrinsic order of the planet, the symbiotic nature of all life and the ever present question of the human purpose within it all. My interests led me to find a valuable network of people of the kind without which I would not have found my way or had the skills and companionship to stay the course. Amidst this we now had a business to run from early morning till late at night and a toddler who had a will of iron. Daily a mini mount Vesuvius erupted and nightly she made it crystal clear that she had a severe allergy to sleep. It was obvious that Saskia was already surfacing in me a questing explorative life that had always been there.

Parenting and being responsible for the caretaking of another life, had shone a strobe light onto everything and new illuminations happened daily. She was teaching me about me and the more I learned and understood the more proactive I yearned to be. What I did not realise was that I would need much self-awareness and training to get to where I was intended, and Saskia would provide a whole classroom of learning experience all by herself.

Children hold a mirror in front of your life and reflect back to you so much of the self- development needed within yourself. Sas had her own little hall of funny mirrors and a sense of timing that was eerily uncanny. The 'Law of Attraction' was fascinating me, but not in the way of bringing material things to me. Instead the dynamic revolved around the potential for growth and refinement and I was buzzing with the mission of attracting qualities. I had set my hat first at 'patience' because running a restaurant and dealing with customers for an average of 14 hours a day demanded a lot of patience.

However my mini mentor was not impressed by being left out of the loop in her mother's quest for saintly patience and decided to show me that without her unorthodox approach to teaching, that bright halo of patience would never be attained. I had barely risen to a new day and consciously assembled my systems to the pursuit in hand when Sas began to wind up like a coiled spring except she seemed to crank it up a notch and do an extra turn just for good measure. Duly the next moment indignation, anger and sheer bloody-minded determination produced the force that spun her round the other way and a momentous melt down puthered out of her. It was like watching the lid pop and the Jack spring from the box. Except it was louder. And longer. And where the hell was the lid? And then I realised, she couldn't contain this and neither could I. Getting stressed trying to 'force the lid back on' just added heat to the lava flow.

What you give out you attract more of. Any 'hot' emotions would create more heat in her, but if I stood and held on to the patience I did have, I would attract more. Patience could not join an impatient heated life. It needed to see the cool balm of itself, its own signal, to add more, to bring more.

A child could not change that state for itself. They needed an adult to find some intactness and way to help them through it. Within 10 seconds of holding that space, and listening to this rush of understandings, I began to feel a warm gentle surge of love that encompassed a core of tolerance and understanding for the little life before me. That day the mini explosive in her fizzled out much quicker and every time I could catch myself and muster all within to patience and peace we both were taken out of the eye of the storm much quicker.

It was many years later that I discovered that the first rush of hormones begins at 2 years old. Every adult has felt at some point powerless to the potent effects hormones cause. How confusing and frightening this is to a small child is difficult to comprehend. I still very much wish I had known that at the time to help me understand her temperament better, but what anchors I lacked in understanding were soon made up for through other channels.

I was not going to be allowed to stray far from the tracks of intention I had declared were important, although now I realise that as I generally travel at the speed of a snail on tranquilizers it was never me who made the choice of what was important to attract. The choice was made important to me by helping hands that knew very well how to switch lights of perception on in my being! Lord knows how they navigate free will at their end of the deal!!

So there came the day where, too frenetic and focused on work, I began meeting Sas's resistance with a general lack of tolerance. The more she made it clear that this approach was most displeasing to her, the more intent I got in me that she would just have to bend to my will. As a strategy for parenting a Saskia it was dumb. And as time management goes it was doomed to failure. I was getting more insistent, resistant and stubborn and she was digging her little heels so hard into the ground the floor boards were wincing. Suddenly the words 'Stop now' boomed through my head. I stood totally still, shocked at the intensity and force of it.

Clearly it required a whole peacekeeping force to pull me out of my battle strategy. The tone and level returned to a more familiar sound. "You must not break this child's will, you must help her to hone it. She needs a strong will for her life's purpose ahead." I had never asked a question consciously before but it was clear and formed in my thoughts before I could stop it.

"How long will it take before she begins to calm down?" The answer came clear and strong "At eight years old she will change. Trust." And duly, when Saskia passed 8 her radiation and temperament very obviously changed. It was a relief to see that settlement for her. And the 'sleep allergy' went away too!

The truthful guidance had become a security blanket of love which continually flooded me with profound realizations. I felt deep gratitude for knowing how natural it is to be accompanied and assisted and to be held in that space where it is so tangibly clear how loved and valued all human life is. The desire and desperation in me multiplied in its wish to enable that source to move closer to all human lives, for many to know of it consciously. I felt it's longing to be with the human as much as the human longing to be with it. The source had been there for me and now the time was emerging when I would be ready to play my part for it.

There is a point where that combined devotion and dedication causes a gate to swing open and you consciously walk through it knowing life will never be the same again. It's exactly what you have worked for, willed for, prayed for and struggled to overcome yourself for. It's a choice you made before you came here, you still don't know what lies in store, all you know is if that choice was allowed then you are capable of meeting it. There is not a single speck in the universe that does not hold the absolute and total passion, will and might of intention that each human life will succeed. And you are one of them. When you pass over that threshold the whole system feels as if it has been plugged into the national grid.

The true pure love that courses through with each new realisation and connection is an agony and an ecstasy to process, to receive. It grows and grows to far more than one life has the virtue or capacity to hold and internally it itches from the base of your spine to be liberated, to be applied, to burst out of you and grow. It built and built and grew in me until something knew I could contain it no more. And then, like a mother to be and a midwife together, one day in unison my companion and I spoke out loud together, "I want to be a Healer." This time we knew together what that moment was about, and we held hands as the lid flew of the chocolate box of life and we dived together into a wealth of training in healing dynamics. I had found what I wanted to do when I grew up. I was 35 years old. And not a coffee cream in sight!

Chapter 3

Stepping into the Future

A cascade of tiny shivers and prickles were coursing up my spine. The eyes had been staring at me for some time. As I scrubbed the soot encrusted bricks inside of the old fireplace the presence moved in closer. With each movement of the now grimy brush I silently spoke with the long departed life. Clearly a masculine energy who deserved careful respect, for he had long occupied this room both whilst living and having passed on, whilst it was barely a week since I had first walked through the front door of this once proud old house. Since then I had scraped the room's walls clean of woodchip and layers of faded wallpaper below. The intended therapy room was calling for a lot of healing of its own, inhaling the energy of care like a newborn taking its first breath.

Another few moments and it would feel right to turn around, to see the owner of the penetrating stare. Years before, bricks and breezeblocks had been carelessly stacked and cemented together blocking the fireplace, denying the room a flow of life that was intrinsic to its very soul. The room knew I would feel every blockage of its arteries and veins and release it from the trauma's human hands wielding breezeblocks and vile Formica cladding had caused it. Every inch of wall had been stifled and skirting boards and door frames torn out to clad the room in a suit of Formica armour. A strait jacket of plastic low maintenance walls that sounded the death knell to painters and decorators of the world and held two fingers up to the realms of good taste and feng shui. With the addition of fluorescent strip lighting the successful creation of a direly unhealthy working environment had been completed. The previous occupants had rolled their 'labour and cost saving' design out across much of the building. They had probably paid out more in sick pay to depressed ailing workers than occasional re-decoration would have cost them.

I could feel the building stretching, sighing, and smiling more each day as the charity workers released every corner of it from its long suffocation. The delight and joy they exuded at creating welcoming and beautiful new surroundings for their clients and for themselves to do their valuable support work filled the building with a new air of hope and happiness.

The house was coming home to itself. Even though it was now late in the evening and I was all alone, covered in soot, I was still rejoicing at being asked to create this space and begin therapy work full time. Pressure mounted in my forehead as my vision moved into the space in the mind where seeing is beyond physical time frames and pictures form you learn to trust, to thread together with an acute awareness of detail.

A short stocky gentleman was standing in the doorway. Aged around 60, he regarded me kindly through small round glasses. Trousers that were close to swallowing him whole were held high with braces and his upper body was clad in a cardigan that he had clearly favoured for some years. He had lived alone and this room was very dear to him. Sensing his feelings transported me into the space he had resided in. The furnishings were sparse and worn through the love of use, his faded arm chair drawn close to the glowing fire and, in front of it, a small table with drawings, detailed exacting sketches he was working on. A canary cheeped and hopped from perch to perch in its cage in the right-hand corner of the window wall, which was decorated with long, faded wallpaper. It was a pattern I recognized as one amidst the many layers I had stripped the previous days. I could see coal miners but knew he wasn't a miner. The mines were a part of him though. Just like cleaning, building and lighting a fire and staring into the glowing embers of this fireplace, the pits had been part of the rhythmic daily heartbeat of this life.

Sometimes there is a surge of relief, of openness, when life, long passed from the physical worlds, finds a receptive moment happening. In that moment can we remember this open door is for them and hold our focus of mind and heart well? It felt special to be allowed into the gentleman's life and for the energetic life of the building, to know I was able to experience its history.

He was smiling his gladness at his home being in good kindly hands. The will of lives wishing it well, making it well, had drawn him in close to watch, to enjoy. When the fireplace had been freed from its cold, hard, dark isolation a tangible air of sadness had lifted. The room devoid of the feature of its life preserving warmth and comfort had caused the gentleman confusion and sadness. But as the currents of energy and vibration returned to their familiar resonance, so too did his vibration recalibrate with it.

As I assured him of our good intentions he wandered onwards and I bade him good evening and left for the night. It came naturally after this to convey to him, and the energetic life of the building, the process of each step. That

I knew the clean plaster would cleanse old prints and the fresh paint would scrub away tired old energy. He seemed to like the gently curving arch framing the fireplace, the new plaster provided, and when we laid a smooth new base and installed a fountain that cascaded down shells he understood the importance of clean running water as a focal point was just as vital as the warmth of the fire had been to him.

The build-up of dirty static energy is vital to avoid in a therapeutic space. Purely by the nature of the work there is a continual detoxing of old energies from both recipients and therapist's systems and man-made fibres, metals and all manner of items will hold on to that exhaust. The atmosphere will then become clogged and unhealthy for clients and practitioners alike creating a space too toxic and dense for fine healing forces to attend and do their work. Because this static exhaust is heavy it sinks to the ground and builds up in corners of the room.

Therefore design and natural materials are important to get right and daily physical and energetical cleaning practices are vital. Clean purified water daily, trickling over the cleansing form of shells and placed at ground level provides a valuable aid to clearing the atmosphere during treatments and a relaxing background too. As so often happens when a building and its prior occupants are heard and treated respectfully there soon came a time when I could sense him no more. But, in true fashion, during a healing one day with a fellow practitioner I was caused to remember that night and remarked that I felt a previous occupant was now at peace with the space. My client opened his eyes a few moments later and said, "He is indeed settled, and all is well. But, by the way, he wants you to know he was a mining manager and did a lot of the technical work for the pits - mining safety, structure etc." I now knew the reasons for the detailed plans. It is always a delight to have the insight of others who are sensitive to the energetic realms and there can often be an artful skill in how those passed lives you meet build your confidence by confirming details that they have shown to you that no one else could possibly know.

I thanked the gentleman for allowing me to be privy to his life, and for helping me too, and my colleague left knowing we would share more interesting times together ahead. Indeed, it would first be within the loving walls of that room with good colleagues such as this, that I would tangibly meet the nature spirits' lives that timelessly maintain and cleanse buildings and land and realise the source of the child like comedic companionship that had begun to join the journey.

Faithful, pure magical lives that would teach me what the previous 16 years of research and exploration and the last years of healing training and work had prepared me for.

Before all that could commence however, I had a room to complete and as generous, and perfect, as the arrangement was for my skills and labour to create a therapeutic space for the charity's clients, and for those who sought me out privately, our budget was slim. The charity supports families and friends whose lives are affected by another's addiction. A tsunami of effects hurtles through lives when a loved one falls into the distress that leads to addictive patterns and the valuable practical ways, insights and connections the charity provides to manage the pain of another's life being taken over by ill health, homelessness, crime and so much more is a rare oasis. Lives with personal experience and big hearts with cool heads that hold a passion for reducing pain, creating space in lives for hope and ways to invite and make change. Their avid intensity at transforming the building into a haven that shone with a quality that reflected the value they held for each life that found the way to their door was miraculously making a palace on a bedsit budget. Meanwhile I was rapidly running short of the skills and money in the allotted pot to make the space as beautiful and functionally correct, as all deserved it to be. I was about to be reminded that landmark moments in my life had never been navigated without guiding hands on the tiller and this time their off-piste route and style would be particularly inventive.

In between running now a busy handmade chocolate business Taeke had laid a long awaited French oak floor in our lounge/dining room. In true old cottage style our home showed its pleasure at the new floor and newly damp proofed walls by demanding a new bath too.

This it conveyed by springing a leak in the old one, which was not one of its brightest plans as that ruined part of the newly plastered kitchen ceiling. I was spending my work and time off amidst general building site chaos and each night a lamp had developed an annoying little mind all of its own and was turning itself on and off. I was too distracted by scratching my head over the budget and costing up the items needed to get beyond it being 'yet another annoyance'. So, beyond Taeke dismantling the lamp and finding no reason for its nightly misbehavior we all ignored both that and the insistent presence in the house. I was particularly obtuse because every time I passed Taeke's Gran's photograph on the stairs her eyes drew me in but I was too preoccupied to do the wise thing and sit with the photograph quietly and ask her why?

However Gran, or Beppe as she had been known, would prove to be extremely artful ahead but meanwhile the frequency and persistence of the lamp's on and off antics increased.

With the therapy room now plastered and painted and plumbing installed, I had a clear vision of a fine porcelain freestanding basin with a retro tap sitting ethereally on a slate base with a granite surround. Having purchased the wood for door frames and skirting boards, which I spent days staining a rich oak shade with walnut and linseed oil ready to be fitted, and a sheet of strong solid wood base in anticipation of the desired basin, my cash box was now even lighter. The eye watering costings of flooring, furniture and numerous small items still to buy stared back at me from the list before me. I could see my vision shrinking to a miniscule cloakroom basin and a row of thin white tiles with some naff dolphin transfers. "I have a champagne vision on lemonade pockets," I sighed, "you need to get your head out of the clouds and get real Sue." The words were no sooner uttered than a sharp stab of indignation prodded me. A surge of disgust flooded me.

Something was not impressed with my defeatist attitude to the mission in hand. The yellow pages phone directory lay before me; the numerous listings of bathroom outlets having been leafed through and only adding to my sense of defeat. Suddenly my eyes were closed, the pages were flicked, and my forefinger had stabbed down forcefully. The store it was on was 20 miles away. I was in the car and driving there before I had time to question. In the past I had experienced my systems following a whole inner intelligence all of their own.

That day their knowledge of the bathroom store was uncanny. Having since had conscious recall of experiencing astral and mental travel I now know that during some hour of the night previously my systems had indeed been taken to this store. And as they are not given to browsing at the best of times, they lead me straight to a corner where an assortment of end of line goods were displayed. In the darkest corner, waiting to be found, sat the perfect modern round basin and desired retro tap for a third of the prices I had seen them at. Barely an hour after my moment of defeat I arrived home triumphantly with my precious purchase.

Sas was enjoying a day off from the assistant manager's job she had at a local bar. Still beautifully wilful and confident, with a keen intuition, she decided we would surf the wave of success and venture out together for the surround. Driving straight to a large tiling outlet, we entered the shop laughing and joking together, and were met by an assistant with sparkling eyes and a very cheeky grin. "Nice to see sisters out together," he winked. "What can I do for you ladies?" "Large slate tiles please," Sas replied with a winning smile and he led us to a shelf sporting a 'Star Buy' sign. At that price I could tile the base and surround. It was, I thought, as good as I could hope for so the assistant duly counted the required number into a box. As he rang up the sale Sas turned to me and said, rather loudly, "The basin will still look nice with slate at the back of it too, Mum. Even those are stretching the charity budget." The assistant swung round from the cash register. "What charity? And budget, for what?" he enquired. So we explained about the work of the charity, the task of transforming the building and my visions for the room, which he listened to with interest, gave us genuine encouragement and wished us well. We had just happily hauled the tiles into the boot of the car when the assistant appeared wheeling a very heavy box on a trolley. "Here you go, girls," he smiled, heaving the box into the boot, "these were a display and have been lying around at the back. By my reckoning these will do the job." Sas and I peered inside the box. There were over a dozen huge black and white solid granite tiles. "But, but these would cost a fortune," I stuttered. His face lit up with a wide smile, "Yep, way too much for a charity budget, love. And way too good to lie around the back getting broken or forgotten about. Better you use them my love and make that great space for those good folk. Enjoy with our compliments."

The kindness in human beings is stunning. I was too overwhelmed to speak. "You'd better take a hug from me and my sister then," cheeked Sas, and having thanked him profusely, we duly left, waving madly with big smiles on all our faces. "That made his day to do that, you know, Mum," Sas said as we drove home. "But it wouldn't have happened if you hadn't come with me," I reflected. "Thank you, treasure, for speaking out!" Sas turned in her chair. "Mum, you work hard and you give a lot of time freely to do good work. People want to help and you are always telling me everyone inside is good. How can they show that if you don't give them a way?"

Thus far I had received 18 years of life skill training from my daughter. Next I was to learn how the universe teaches many lessons in one and be reminded about the law of attraction – ask and you will receive!

Chaos was abating. New bath in place, ceiling repaired, and Brenda, a great friend with amazing skills had offered her time to tile around the precious basin. Only the lamp continued its on and off antics. I passed down the stairs, Beppe's eyes following me all the way. "We do think of you," I told her as I wandered into the lounge. Two minutes later

I was lifting my feet to study my wet socks. Three minutes later I was staring in shock at a slowly dripping radiator valve. Tentatively I pressed my toes against the edge of a floorboard. Water seeped up between the oak boards.

Having invested in extra thick underlay to create a cozy floor over the pitch mastic base, we had succeeded in providing a sponge that had been soaking the slow drip up for weeks. And in that moment I knew exactly how many weeks. Exactly the amount of weeks the lamp had been flashing its warning at us. Beppe had tried so hard to warn us before the floor was ruined and I had ignored every clue. Taeke had worked so hard to skillfully lay the floor and Beppe must have proudly watched him. She would have listened and heard his mind tuning in to his Dad's skill as a joiner. When he cut the wood perfectly around the irregular stone fireplace. Between his and unseen hands he had mastered the task beautifully knowing his work was accompanied.

I didn't know whom I felt most saddened for and I felt completely stupid for ignoring Beppe's insistent warnings. Yet again the kindness in human beings responded amazingly and within hours the insurance company had arranged payment for a new floor direct to the shop and a fitter was dispatched to lift the wrecked boards and underlay. My optimism dented at yet another watery disaster, I busied myself moving furniture and delaying Brenda's help with tiling. Feeling behind schedule, and questioning my sorry lack of intuition, I closed the lounge door, blocking the site of the fitter lifting the soaked floor, lost in a stream of unhelpful conflicting thoughts.

Suddenly the fitter burst through the lounge door breaking through the little whirlpool of negativity I was observing my inner lives battling with. It was like being between a jostling mass of children in a kindergarten. Whilst certain neurons and hormones seemed hell bent on thoughts and feelings that visually resembled toddlers throwing down their toy bricks in disgust, others seemed to be examining each one and calmly working out how the pieces fitted together. Only I, the "me" amidst all this, could focus and unite them but my self-responsibility department was taking an extended tea break. Sometimes, however much self-awareness and life skill you have won, the lushness of going on strike and complaining just takes centre stage. The fitter's next words quietened the cacophony like a bag of dummies being plugged into a row of screaming babies' mouths. "Half the floor is intact, love. Come and take a look." I stared at the perfect line in the underlay the moisture had seeped to in disbelief. "It's all got to be lifted and a whole new one laid, it's paid for and authorized. But you've got a fair whack of perfect underlay and boards here, do you want me to put them separate?" Did I? Half the floor, over £500 worth of beautiful oak wood flooring for a waiting therapy room....and of course exactly perfect in size for what was required!

Crossing the entry 'Floor – how to afford?' off my ever-decreasing list of requirements and trilling with the feelings of joy and thanks for the mystery of life's order, I carefully stacked the rescued boards in dust sheets. Some very testing negatives had been rebalanced by incredibly engineered positives, and I'd got to learn to keep the faith, put things in perspective and plough on!

As I wrapped the underlay around the precious cargo tears of thanks and apology ran down my cheeks. It felt like a hundred arms were hugging me and an orchestra of wise knowing essences were balming the whole of me.

They know our weaknesses and our strengths and they love us for the whole of what we are. Within pure love lives eternal forgiveness and endless acceptance. What matters is that we try, that we pursue what's in our hearts and dreams and we accept the learning along the way. They read intently our intentions and will us to ever greater purposes. For with the desire to see all lives valued, from the burning wish to see all flourish and know they are loved, and moved by the powers of healing to work to transform hurt, loneliness and pain, we join their purpose. We become alive to the joy and purity of their feelings and the powerful force for humanity to know how rich and connected to the whole its destiny is. The mellow balm of their healing reconnected all the inner thoughts and feelings like a needle on a compass lining up due north.

With internal Lego bricks stacked seamlessly again, and the self-responsibility department back on duty, I felt the last of the dummies drop sheepishly back into the bag! Another lesson learned. Just a few days later, with Brenda's endless skills and generosity of time, the basin proudly stood on its slate base encircled by the lush granite surround. With ingenuity, and great joy at the salvage, she had also skillfully laid the floor and Taeke had completed the transformation, fitting the matching oak-stained skirting boards and door frames. The cash box now feeling veritably rich to purchase just furniture, we moved in one week to a completed room and an intact dry home. As I surveyed the room, completed just as I had visualized, a little voice broke through. "The Universe are Master Distillers you know?" "Sorry, what?" I asked puzzled. "They have made you champagne from lemonade." "Yes. Yes they have." I laughed. And, vowing to monitor my thoughts a whole lot closer, I bade the mischievous friend good night and headed for home. I had a Beppe to talk with!

Placing Beppe's photograph on the table, I had just lit a candle and created a suitable space physically and in my mind, when Sas dashed through the door from work in a flurry of excitement. We did not need a degree in psychology to see she was bursting to tell us something. "You will not believe what happened tonight," she began, "there was a medium show, and I was listening in from behind the bar, she was really good. Lots of people had received messages and then she said she had a lady who was very insistent to talk to Sue, but there was no Sue in the audience. So she asked for more details but couldn't understand her name. The lady said she passed on from bowel cancer and she had been trying to tell Sue about a leak. The medium said the lady was very concerned because there had already been a leak which had ruined a ceiling and the house had been in a mess with workmen and she wanted to get Sue's attention to this other leak. I had to tell her she was totally right, and the message was for my Mum. I explained that it was Beppe from Holland, who did pass from bowel cancer, and she had been trying to warn us by turning a lamp on and off for weeks. The audience was impressed and the medium understood then why she couldn't recognize her name with it being Dutch. That is pretty amazing isn't it?"

I was staring at Sas, stunned.

Just lately she had really been swept up into the extraordinary. She was clearly ready to understand much more of the worlds I was so used to trusting and knowing as real. Sas was staring at the photograph and lit the candle. "Are you talking with Beppe, mum" she asked. Deciding that it was a good time to offer an explanation, we opened a bottle of wine and sat down together. "I need to explain to you why this photograph is so powerfully connective. To do that I need to tell you a true story. And I want to tell you this now because you are ready to understand that life is extraordinary and passing over is purely a continuance.

"Those we love are always close when they can be, their love continues and they find ways to tell us, to express that, even though they no longer have a physical form to express that thought. We are born here from the energy worlds, miraculously arriving into a physical body and when we pass over we purely leave that physical body behind, for it belongs to Earth, whilst we are temporary visitors here. It will be that we come here many times because we have a lot to learn and to experience creation in its physical form it has managed, to date, to manifest on this very special unique planet is a rare gift to be allowed to try. Life has form here, so what we see, touch, taste, hear and smell on earth can only be experienced fully through a physical form. And we are here to experience it, explore it, and discover it, on behalf of what caused it to be.

"And on behalf of what caused us to be too. At core we are all one, all humans, all nature, all life, and the universe. You and I, every human being is never ever truly alone.

"And once you understand that life is never the same. What you see, hear, sense and experience is different, what you can intend and do is different. And it carries a responsibility. I put careful intention into everything I do so there is a reason why her photograph allows such a flow of connection. When Beppe passed I did a special healing ceremony through this picture. To explain why I need to tell you of a very potent process I was involved in with about 100 other people a few years ago."

With wine glasses replenished and appreciating the peace, night time and an intact house provides, we settled down together. Hugging Sas, and thanking the Angels for the daughter gifted us, I began, knowing that Beppe too would enjoy this time with us together. "I was at a seminar where we learned about the process of passing over. Everyone there held good intent and was open and willing to do whatever work that was needed. Purely the nature of our gathering and collective agreement caused a lot of interest from lives who had passed and the room was filling up more each day with energy and presences. On the third day we spent the morning preparing very thoroughly. Sometimes lives pass and need extra power to enable them to get to where they are intended to next be.

"People can move on and work in all sorts of ways in the next planes of life. It is all determined by the life that's been lived here, how they pass over and numerous other factors too. We were shown how to project energy from our solar plexus, we went through a long process of preparation of ourselves and the room, and within that we were asked to have two people in mind to first invite in to help. If they did not come then we would know they were wherever they were meant to be. As everyone focused and intended, the room filled up more and more with people needing help. It brought home to me yet again that thoughts are powerful and what you intend you must follow through with and do. For the first few minutes nothing happened with me. The two lives I had in mind did not come. Thus, I knew wherever they were it was meant to be. Being stacked up with energy to give I simply asked if there was anyone else who knew me that needed help. Within seconds two people appeared before me. One was a beautiful vivacious young friend whom I had sent healing to religiously, and written letters to, daily during her times in hospital. The cancer did not allow her to live beyond her 20's and when she passed I avidly worked in myself to send her onwards to her next life with happiness and joy knowing I could change my sadness and wanting her to be helped on her journey. Healing has many faces and forms to honour, to hear and to allow. To see her before me, young, smiling, captivatingly beautiful was incredible. I felt she knew I could hold the integrity further. It was an honour to be allowed."

"And right next to her was Pake, Beppe's husband, Earth years on from passing over. Of course Beppe then was still alive here. Anyway, I had to press on with the promise they had both responded to, so I asked Pake to bear with me, looked straight at my beautiful young friend and said, 'I love you so much. Take this energy, take all you need and fly treasure, fly.' I could feel the energy power into her and her receive it. She didn't need much, and within 2 minutes I could feel her leaving and the energy dying down.

"So I turned my focus on Pake who needed a lot more to power him on. He was still sitting in his chair, in his lounge, just sitting there looking at me. He was fond of that chair bless him, but he had clearly remained earth bound and had missed his window to walk through after he passed. But, after about 5 minutes of feeling this pure energy course through my solar plexus and pass into him, he suddenly just stood up, gave me a lovely smile and walked across the room. He walked straight through the window and disappeared. It was like he had the power to break out of the walls and place he had lived in for so long. I sent more energy for a few minutes to be sure he had plenty of fuel for his trip and then naturally the force died down and my systems began to settle from the fizzing energy that had been coursing through them."

Sas drained the bottle into our glasses. Was I right to tell her this? "Carry on, mum" she said impatiently! "Ok. Well, around me everyone else too was coming out of the process and the energy was audibly reducing that we had all been united by and with. The room felt emptier and I was sure many lives had also benefitted that none of us knew. My legs were wobbly so I backed into a chair, but just as I reached it and sat down I felt the softest, most familiar wool against my cheek and neck and arms were encircling me tight. The last hug I ever had with my friend she was wearing that jumper. I energetically hugged her back with all my might. It was the most beautiful sensation, the most tangible real perfect hug and the most beautiful gift to give me. That moment is etched on my memory forever. And then she spoke, her voice so clear next to my ear, *'Thank you Sue, thank you!'* I knew every effort, every try had helped her and now, this ceremony had given her all she needed to do what she was intended to do. *'I love you darling. Now fly, be happy. See you again someday.'* I had fulfilled my friendship and she had given me more in that hug to motivate me onwards in my work than she would ever perhaps know."

"So did everyone help someone that day, Mum?" Sas asked. "Everyone I spoke with had stunning stories to tell. Many had spoken with the lives who came to them and they gave details that were personal which was very emotional for them to hear. Some even apologized for not believing in life beyond and being critical of their friends' or relatives' beliefs. When healing flows it always brings equal return. It's the most giving generous force for good one could ever have the privilege to meet and give service to." "So, when Beppe passed were you trying to make sure she did not get stuck in her home like Pake did?" I nodded cautiously, we were both close to tears and as much as I did not want to make Sas cry I knew too well that tears can bring their own healing. Often they are the only way emotions can express and let go of hurts and wounds that can become harmful if buried or not given a chance to surface in a safe and remedial way. Squeezing her tightly I continued, "Beppe needed to pass on. Her last two years were not pleasant or kind. As those we love do, her family willed her to have treatments and live on. She 'chose' a time to go when your Dad was in Holland and he did the most honourable thing any life can do for another. He sat with her and gave her permission to go. It was brave and very beautiful to do. I needed to honour that in him and I wanted Beppe to move away from the pain and illness as quickly as possible and be with Pake. What if I had helped him and she couldn't reach him? So I created a healing space and the channel of communication was instantly clear."

"But how did you manage to speak when your Dutch is not fluent and Beppe had no English at all?" "Now *that* was the most fascinating thing, Sas. My thoughts left my head, my mind in English *but* I could hear her receive them in perfect Dutch. Language cloaks a frequency, just like red, orange, yellow etc. each has a frequency of its own when it appears here yet all colour is inside of white, so too must each language represent a frequency and beyond a certain point all language must be united. Somewhere beyond the earth plane of physicality there is a point of no difference. It made me wonder about the Tower of Babel in the Bible and whether that story is from a time when either the vibration on Earth changed or the human form changed. It made me sure that before then we did not communicate verbally but instead through the mind telepathically.

"Maybe that is also how knowledge, beliefs and skills travelled huge distances. People did not have to physically travel for religious beliefs, ways of creating communities and building skills to pass onwards. Instead the same intention made connections. Perhaps that is what is meant by 'being of like mind'. It was remarkable and I knew it all travelled to her clearly. And I think she was grateful and wanted to help us in return but I stupidly ignored all her tries."

For a while we sat quietly together, both thinking of Beppe, it had somehow worked out to be more perfect than any ceremony alone would have been. Eventually Sas stretched and, wiping her eyes, stood and walked to the door. "Well, it's been one intense night of learning, Mum, and do you know what? I think Beppe made sure I heard her communicate through that medium too. She made sure so that you would be believed. She's pretty clever, is Beppe, don't you think?" "I am surrounded by clever people," I laughed. And Sas headed off to bed. "Time for Sas to rest those very perceptive faculties," I said to Beppe's photograph. "Bless you and thank you, Beppe. Time I think to pop you back on the stairs." Her gaze became more penetrating with each step I took, her message could not have been clearer this time. Doubling back to the lounge I positioned her carefully amongst the many family photos on the dresser. Her energy settled. My first lessons in the power of photographs, lights and fireplaces as potent points of manifestations and communications was complete. So without further ado the universe decided to introduce me personally to its many planetary healing elementals and lives. And my! Were these realms eager to teach me!!

Chapter 4

The First Dance with the Air Spirits

The Elemental Waltz

I swirl, I spin, I cleanse, I purify.

I, the life of air, remove coarseness as I fly.

I serve our Hostess Earth, and humans, day and night.

See my purifying breath, cooling, sweeping, transforming dull to bright. Who knows us? Prince and Princess of Invigorating clean,

A part of Earth, her faithful kidneys, we serve our Lady, our Queen.

Her reverence and our purpose endure,

But can we awaken human consciousness too? Yes, we sense a life who knows us.

Today an Elemental will waltz with you.

***

The whirling energy had a life of its own. Its dance graceful, gentle, holding me safely in an embrace that allowed my feet to defy gravity and my eyes to sparkle and shine with tears.

These were the cradling arms of a long lost dear friend. Our combined energy pulsed with exhilaration and the communion of two intelligences exchanging greetings, signals and messages way beyond a place where physical words and senses inhabit.

It felt as natural as breathing to partner this elemental life. Somehow I knew it. Somewhere deep within me something knew and was drinking in the sensations and vibrations of communication like scorched parched earth receiving crystal cool raindrops. The client lay peacefully sleeping on the couch as together we cleansed and cleaned blockages in the energy field around him. Three spirited lives, free of confines and inner and outer noise, locked in a sacred cleansing dance. Our spirits unfettered, liberated, joyous, for this is how it is meant to be. It had been building to this moment for weeks. Each time I had worked cleansing and clearing blockages in clients' auras, the vibrations, registrations and knowings had become more intense and clear. Often I had felt something lead me and compel me to points and places and cause me to work in a particular way. I had been 'under instruction' from this teacher for weeks. Soon I would discover each element has its teachers and they were queuing up to instruct!

However, today, the resonance of the room and its human occupants were perfectly pitched to welcome the air elemental to show itself fully. The client held a deep passion for nature and our combined open minds and earlier conversation, which had carried our appreciation of the finer, more subtle lives of Earth, had been an invitation the elemental could not resist. They yearn for that chance to reconnect with human kind.

Our combined conversation had moved into a frequency which I could hear and register and transmit from consciously too. We had almost circled around the entirety of the client's aura and had arrived at two points below and to the sides of his feet. It was definitely the elemental who had shown me that the kidneys radiated to these points and I realised had been cleansing and regulating the energy of numerous clients' kidneys and organs. Elementals are masters at cleansing auras, but then they ceaselessly do this work in the hours of the night for us all whilst we sleep. Its energy was buoyant and effervescent, clearly enjoying its work being appreciated and seen.

I realised the elemental was female, and as the thought transmitted she pulsed, causing her vibration to elevate in brightness. Into the range of my vision came a hovering iridescent blue swirling form. A pure vibrant coiled spiral, taller than I, in an almost filament, conical shape. My mind pitched out signals of appreciation "Wow, you are beautiful. I have never seen such a radiant blue." Mental snap shots were happening at speed. This had to be the most vivid moment yet with the Earth's faithful workers and the whole sense of her being made me understand deeper why I felt such a powerful appreciation of Mother Earth. Here with me was a part of her own inner lives, youthful, pure, innocent and willing to connect.

The symbolic harmony of all nature, if allowed to be, adheres to a unity of purpose and balance in extraordinary ways. There is an overpowering sense of appreciation that the Earth and the universe holds for the maintenance realms, that work tirelessly to try to cleave to that mission. Inside of that the work of elementals is like angels' kisses to our now over heating planet.

Ceaselessly they clean land and lives of toxins and coarse force, taking cool, clean, pure energy and vitality wherever they can reach and carry away the dirty and tired, heated, static waste.

The more that hot, low, coarse force emits and builds up from electricity, manufacturing, mobile phones, computers, transmitters and nuclear plants etc. and the natural cycle of night and darkness is overridden by 24-hour industry, commerce and 21st century lifestyles the more difficult, unhealthy and unpleasant the imperative work of the elementals becomes.

In the absence of awareness, or giving serious recognition to this profound and massive realm, the Industrial revolution has driven pollution and static heat to relentless lengths. A huge powering force which, like all life, seeks to grow, for its prospect is to either grow or wither. A force that, without human direction, responsibility and choices made, can only continue to consume and destroy in serving its own self. Lest we escape from our own ignorance or arrogance, it will be the master that as a civilization we serve. Perhaps not as sophisticated and emancipated as we would wish to believe we are.

For the elementals, who cleanse like our kidneys, it is like inhabiting a body that drinks alcohol and consumes chemicals 24 hours a day whilst breathing in tankfuls of petrol fumes through a mask. The task is now endless with little job satisfaction – cities and towns, so much of Earth, is too polluted and heated for the elementals to cleanse and survive to tell the tale. The stoical, generous, gentle sense of love and giving within the elemental gave me hope and stabbed at my heart with shame and sadness all at the same time. She told me her name. I knew it well. She told me how we had known each other for a very long time. I knew this too.

But it absorbed into a part of my subconscious that no amount of meditative coaxing later would allow me to access. When the time was right I would be allowed.

Then she led me over to the wall, asked me to wait and she was gone. I held the moment, held my breath, willing the return of her whirring beauty.

The client slept on. My aura trilled and fizzed as the elemental returned. She guided my hand and again I was whirling inside of the elemental waltz. It was like taking the client's aura through the giant brushes of a car wash. His radiation would sparkle for months after this! But, within a few twirls I realised that what had begun to lead was different. This was a smaller, more tentative elemental. I was dancing with her child. "She is beautiful. I don't want her to be afraid." The powerful protection a mother feels for her child is true throughout creation and I felt huge waves of safety and security emitting from me towards this little junior elemental. "She has never met a human before," her mother pulsed. My protective vibes tripled. "With you she is safe." The lump in my throat felt like a boulder. "I am glad you know that. That you feel that."

I said finally, "Thank you for your trust. And thank you, treasure, for coming to meet me. It is an honour." We whirred around together, the little elemental growing in confidence and exuberance and the frivolity that inhabits all happy children. I love to dance but this was the best dance I would ever have. Her young vitality and vibrancy spun on and on. The three of us could have danced into her adulthood, the experience was so rare and special for us all.

Finally the client stirred. "What time is it?" he asked. The little elemental froze. Wrapping an arm around her I sent her calm, protective words and energy. She relaxed and stayed still.

Glancing at the clock I realised we had been absorbed in the dance for over an hour. He stretched and jumped off the couch, "Wow I feel *great.* But the chicken I left in the oven for dinner might be a little well done!" Apologies were well accepted, as were my tentative explanations about the workers who had made him feel so amazing. With a visibly sparkling aura, and a spring in his stride, the gentleman left to check out his well-cooked dinner. 'He will sleep like a baby tonight,' I thought as I returned to the therapy room.

As I had hoped the two elementals were still there. "Thank you so much for all your hard work and teaching. You've shared so much with me and I hope it's been as much of a joy for you both as it has for me. I must cleanse the room now and go home as it is very late." I could tell the elementals were going nowhere in a hurry. Clearly they knew my routine and were delighted to stay.

So, whirring and spinning they navigated the room whilst I wiped the floor and freshened the area and the linen. The sheets and pillows seemed neater on the couch, the floor more polished, even the walls looked pristine clean. As I lit the charcoal to sprinkle the incense on to purify the atmosphere, I could sense the elementals hum with contentment. Clearly they were attracted by the clean, calm and energetically cool space of the therapy room and the purifying completion the incense provided.

As I walked around the room allowing the incense to puther high into the corners, the elementals spun on ahead, expanding and contracting, whirling dervishes of power, until the atmosphere in the room was as fresh and crisp as mountain air. It was intoxicating. My whole body felt as if it had been dipped in pure spring water and scrubbed till it glowed. We came to a stop, united in satisfaction at a job well done together.

"Bless you both, a million times over. *That* is the *best* cleanse I have ever experienced. You are amazing. Please tell all the elementals how grateful I am for what you do." They pulsed as they received the thanks. "It's just farewell I'm sure," I said to them. "Until very soon," the mother elemental transmitted, "it has been a joy for us too, a delight for all elementals. What we experience so too do all of our kind too."

After a parting whirl, that made me energetically spin and smile, for days, the elementals went onwards to their ceaseless work. Grounding the systems in me that drive the car, I kept the rest of my whole with the memory and recall of the whole experience.

In times ahead I would experience the power and enormity of many elementals working together in ways and tasks that I could never have anticipated would happen. As always the source had ensured a sound and tangible fully conscious first meeting in preparation for what was to come. I would never look to the skies again and see the birds spiraling across the sky, without sending gratitude and love to the elementals who enabled them to rest their wings in flight. The value of cleansing had attained a whole new level and there it would stay.

Chapter 5

Healing with the Earth Spirits

The Elf and Pixie Choir
Allow yourself a quiet space. Travel to woods, forests and glens. Let the child within off the lead. Let it guide you to our dens.

Inside the cave, beside a rock, hiding behind flower and tree. We, the spirited life of earth await. Are you ready to meet me?

Deep within roots, high in the branches, the dryad stretches and creaks.

Spirits of the trees, of deciduous and evergreen, to which do you urge to speak? To strong oak, from whom endurance, stamina and will surge and power.

Or, to flowing, graceful, watery willow who will cleanse with leafy shower.

Perhaps the warmth of the cherry tree can enliven you with her glow.

Or sacred Rowen can shelter you, for she is a tree of protection you know? Maybe the almond tree can delight your eyes with delicate blossom of pink.

So many trees, so many types and each with their character distinct.

For within the tree the dryad stretches and creaks the bough and bow. Waiting, watching, urging shoot and leaf. Is it the dryads you'd like to know? Or do you step lightly into fairy rings and blink and deny their presence?

Do you feel the lightness sparkle, yet deny the effervescent fairy essence?

Have you glimpsed for a moment a sparkling, pirouetting silver triangle in the tree? And as twilight falls, and moon light cascades, have you felt the woods break free? Would you like to see the fairy? Look, there in the oak within a blue ball.

Sits quietly a fairy. If you wait, be still, then you'll see them all.

Interconnected blue balls of light draped from tree to tree.

Yes, that's where fairy lights came from. Now this is the real fairies you see. Was that what you came for, or did you seek a pixie or elf?

You seem to be delighted, so perhaps now you're not so sure yourself No matter, sit with us, listen now, for we have so very much to do.

Today you will meet the pixies and elves and they have much to say to you!

***

I blinked my eyes faster and faster. My eyelids were flickering like a camera shutter. It made not an iota of difference. Sight had moved into energy mode and what I was seeing was not going to change. There, busily and diligently amidst a repair job were a group of little beings. The intense interest in the client's right knee and their deft skill in their work were prompting a whole train of questions in my mind. Either they sensed my awakened awareness of them, or my incredulous stare. I just could not blink anymore, because in unison they looked at me. Tiny perfect features with expectant wide eyes glanced, shot me looks up and down and then returned their focus back to the task in hand. Just one broke away from the group and moved closer to me. Different to his companions, he was stocky in his short stature and distinctly curious to look at, but oddly familiar. "Well," he shouted, nodding his head authoritatively at me "Don't just stand there, we've got work to do!"

Wow! This guy was in charge clearly. And used to being listened to and obeyed! "What are you doing?" I asked lamely. My work, my whole life, had taken on a whole new bizarre level of connection that was proving challenging to talk about around the dinner table! I had sensed a lot at work in healings and regularly glimpsed shapes, forms and lights out of the corners of my eyes in all sorts of places, but had never anticipated anything would come into my vision and experience as clearly as the elemental. And now I was witnessing a scene from elves and the shoemakers, except these were the surgical team!

The little guy rose to his full height which barely topped 6 inches. His wrinkled features took on a distinctly more displeased frown. "What do you think we are doing? There's an old injury in that knee." His tiny index finger jabbed in the direction of his co-workers. "Who do you think does all this work? And how do you think you sense it when you're working? We do the physical repair work. We know the physical forms of every being. Because we are *of* the Earth. Masters and mistresses of physical repair." Hands on hips he stared at me, clearly unimpressed by my previous obtuse behavior. "Oh Kay," I said slowly, "I just have never seen you or the work being done so clearly before. I'm sorry. Just a bit surprised." His stare continued, unchanged. I had better stop my excuses because they were not going to wash with this feisty little chap. "The thing is," I continued, "I'm confused why you're focusing on his knee when he has come with a trapped shoulder? Not that I'm not grateful you are." I hastily added. A sound of impatience huffed loudly from him. He shot me a look that said, "I thought you would be bloody brighter than this," and then comically sat down on the client's thigh swinging his legs vehemently.

I silently prayed the gentleman would stay asleep. The last time this client had come he had confirmed the settled presence of the mining manager so I knew he was very aware and attuned to the energy realms. I was not sure if it extended to nature spirits though.

"I have just told you that we do the physical work. Do you not realise that shoulder is not physically hurt? That is the pain of a trauma. It's trapped, blocked, stuck. That's your job." Now this was making sense. "Right, I understood that, got it loud and clear. But there is a communication issue, a wiring issue, somewhere in this because he has tried to work out what the root of the pain is and he can't access it. He's double trapped!" Leaning closer I tried to look wise. "Do you think there is anything you can do so the message gets through?" "Oh piffle." The words were spat out with an air of humour. "I guarantee he just doesn't want to know. I'll make sure everything's awake in there." And in the blink of an eye he had scampered up the client's body and began shouting in his ear.

I wanted to laugh. Instead, I pinched myself, *hard*. This was surreal yet happening as clear as day. And the strangest thing was, it felt perfectly normal! The pinch was as ineffective as the blinking. It changed nothing. Except the portly little being had stopped shouting in the client's ear. "Everything is wide awake and physically peachy in there, missy. He is just not listening to his own body's intelligence. Now YOU do something." With arms folded, and cheeks pink from the shouting he resumed a very firm stance and stared crossly at me. This was clearly not a request, it was an order. Many times in the healing I had been instructed in a very sudden and almost impatiently bossy fashion. I recognized the tone and had a distinct suspicion I was looking at one of the sources of the cheek and one liners I regularly had interrupting my thoughts. I knew I was groaning inwardly. As much as I knew how endearing and mischievous these realms were, I also knew they were very straight talking and could read every thought I had.

The client stirring and opening his eyes shifted our focus. "What exactly," he enquired, "is happening?" I took an evasive course first. "What are you aware of happening?" He scratched his head, clearly gathering his thoughts, "Well. There's something being done to my knee. Has been for some time. Feels like it's being repaired inside. And as you haven't got a hand near it and I can still feel that it's kind of interesting." He looked at me with an air of anticipation. It was yet again my turn to speak and the only way out was the truth. God only knew what the little guy would do if I didn't just get on with it. 'Any more days like these and I will go and work in an office.' I mentally shot at my bossy mentor. His laughter rang through my ears and I couldn't help but laugh too.

"It's nature spirits," I announced confidently. "They are doing one heck of a repair on your knee. And one has been shouting in your ear." The client was laughing. This was it. The day had come when someone would call the men in white coats to take me away. I hoped the little guy would deliver me a file to pick the lock. "They are *great,* aren't they? I've seen all sorts of planetary energy life." His laughter was happiness, not disbelief! My breath rushed out of me that fast I nearly blew the tiny Boss man over. "Great," I ploughed on, with relief apparent, and trying hard to ignore the indignant glare I was receiving from our small companion. "Well, he's really done a fine job of making sure everything physically is willing to let you access this emotion, this trauma, that's trapped in that shoulder and causing the pain. So settle down into a peaceful space and tell your systems you're ready to know it and release it."

Without hesitation the gentleman lay back down and within minutes his whole body visibly relaxed. I was really beginning to enjoy being in the nature spirits' presence. They worked so thoroughly and avidly and seemed to enjoy being busy and intent on their tasks. The acute sensing of the client's systems was second nature to the Earth spirit. His being just seemed to naturally register each muscle and sinew as it relaxed. I watched, fascinated, as his eyebrows twitched slightly with each inner adjustment. His eyes twinkled with mischief and I tried to focus on those and block the thoughts of how unusual and very slightly ugly he looked to me. I received a flash of, "You humans can look darn weird to us too, Missy," before he leapt back to beside the client's ear. He so had the upper hand. I really had *got* to get a handle on my thoughts. Suddenly the tiny index finger was raised in the air. "He's got it! Well about time. Come on troop, we have got a lot of other work to do elsewhere." I had barely acknowledged the other workers who had completed the knee repair and were poised for other missions.

"Excuse me," I intercepted, "before you go. I'm sorry if I've seemed rude, I didn't mean to be.

And thank you for all the work you do. I'm glad I'm seeing how your healing energies work." Their expressions were open and innocent. Not an ounce of emotion seemed to emanate from them. They truly were very physical based beings, excellent at physical work, physical repairs and childlike in their character. It was a sense of 'Take me as I am because what I am is everything you see.' I totally fell in love with the open honesty. It was the most refreshing engagement to sense and be with I had ever had.

The Boss man was pursing his lips. It seemed to be his thinking pose. "Hmm," There was a pause. The line of his face and lips softened a little. "Good. Makes a damn fine change to be noticed. You'll get used to us. Got a whole lot of us yet to meet. We'll be back. Cause you humans need us. You're not bad though, have to say." My lord, it felt like Einstein had just told me I was intelligent!

The client awakening and sitting bolt upright distracted me from the group. And when I glanced back they were gone. "I've got it!" a wider smile I had rarely seen. "And," he continued "I know exactly what I am meant to do to confirm this totally and finally to myself. I have over 50 Angel cards out there with different directions on them. I know I am now going to pick 'Let it Go' from the pack because I now know I can!" He had dashed out and was back again before I could register fully what was happening. In his hand lay one card with the words 'Let it Go' clearly printed across it. "Went straight to the pack and picked this out. Amazing. Right, come on, let's really help this shoulder to free up. I know you can bring in the help to settle this once and for all."

I was beginning to feel dizzy. Everything and everyone seemed to believe in me a whole lot more than I believed in myself. Pushing the doubts and thoughts aside, I mentally thanked the healing realms for yet another day of the bizarre but wonderful and began to place all my attention to summoning help to free him of the emotional pain fully. I had no need to know the detail of it. There is a finite timing to when a trauma or deep distress can be uncovered when a person's systems have locked it away from conscious access.

Everything works to protect itself from pain, but then the physicality can become distressed and affected. Once it has become conscious again, or troubles our thoughts and feelings repeatedly, it must be relegated and settled. Trauma and hurts and wounds can lodge in all sorts of places in the body. And whilst there are numerous physical injuries and pains from physical wear and tear, all of them will have an emotional or physical aspect to them. Many pains will exclusively radiate and persist from traumas or distressing events in life.

The human systems are incredibly tidy at trying to insulate the damage and limit the impact and effect any emotional hurt causes. When persistent pain sets in, it is a way the body points to try to get attention to the issue. But sometimes the connection to the root of it takes some work to find. There is even a sequence to where each specific emotion is lodged. So, the kidneys will hold fears, whilst anger will lodge in the liver and grief and uncertainty will affect the lungs. Discovering the relationships between different emotions and organs and systems causes huge respect for the intelligence of the human design and enables a therapist to work in a harmonious way with the whole. However the more you discover, the more you realise there is to learn!

The body works tirelessly day and night on our behalf and, just like the Earth's nature spirits, doctors, surgeons and nurses are incredibly skilled at physical repair and comfort. But, as we are emotional, intuitive and instinctive beings also, the human systems need to be treated and supported in those inner lives too. I would never have the skill or bravery to be a surgeon, and would not wish to be one, however like most fellow humans I had been given 5 senses, plus a human system to learn through. The more work I did, the more I saw and sensed and heard and even smelled. Empathy and awareness of worlds that had been unseen and beyond senses, became normal for my every sense to register in an enhanced and new way. The *peace* in the healing room was so intense I could hear its presence. A clear penetrating whistle that pierced my ears and through the centre of my brain. It was stunning but slightly painful at the same time. The client was deeply relaxed and surrendering to the potency of the force. With mind intent to the need and purpose my whole body began to tremble and quiver with force.

This was stronger than I had felt it before. Whatever assistance had arrived it had come from a very high source. My hands were ice cold and the atmosphere was like cool crystal glass, visually sparkling. As blasts of cold force emitted from my fingertips, I placed them firmly on each of the client's shoulders and mentally projected for the pain to be taken away. Above the couch a pristine radiant light of the most pure varied colours shaped itself before my eyes into a diamond shape. The fine energy pulsed with force, a vibration passed through the gentleman and the diamond shrank back and disappeared. Its power was astonishing and the speed of it appearing and disappearing had been less than a minute.

I was still staring open mouthed when the client caught my eye silently mouthing, "Wow."

Neither of us moved. We simply stayed in the tranquil, pure, balming atmosphere staring at the ceiling, silently acknowledging that we would forever know what it meant to be 'Graced with a Presence.' Eventually the spell broke and he sat up. "A portal," he gasped "I have never before seen a diamond shaped portal! It took the residual pain straight out of me. Everything in me just surrendered, gave it up. That *was stunning*. What an honour! My God, thank you, Sue. Thank you, Essences and Nature Spirits."

I had to sit down. My legs had turned to jelly. The vivid picture of the portal was clear in my mind and the atmosphere was still serene. I'd got to gather my thoughts together. Some things needed to be declared whilst still in the presence of the healing grace. Plus it felt like I had knotted spaghetti where my brain had been! Talking this out would unknot the wiring and hopefully then my brain would once again feel like a fully functioning network of connections not a bowl of pasta.

Sinking a glass of water in a few gulps, I straightened up and smiled at the client who had also pulled up a chair. "Today I'm certain of 3 things. One is that neither the Nature Spirits nor the Essence healing within that portal could have come today and done their work without your genuineness and openness and belief. The second is I feel humbled and glad to know better, much better and deeper and clearer *what* actually does this work and what is facilitated and given chance by my belief, our belief, so that it can work its wonders and miracles. But I think most importantly I now really understand that for every part of that realm we have seen, there will have been hundreds of others working their magic that we haven't yet seen or realised. And I need them to know that we are grateful and glad. I feel they have enjoyed this as much as we both have, and I'm grateful for their trust, and for yours too."

After some further quality time with the energies, we exchanged hugs and the gentleman swiveled his shoulder without a wince. "Awesome, and my knees in fine shape too!" Glowing with vigour he walked to the door and then stopped and turned. "You forgot something earlier. You forgot that you have worked hard, and work hard, every day to attract those healing elementals and essences. So when you count your blessings, count yourself in too. You owe it to yourself and to them." There is something very profound about the openness and honesty that can happen in the presence of healing and fine energies.The human is made to be expressive and genuinely able to communicate from deep within.

The exchange of value, gratitude and appreciation takes on a heartfelt but unfussy and uncluttered clarity and in those spaces and moments a kinship of equality and human companionship appears that nothing can taint or take away from. It's a moment when humanity is reached, when difference shifts from its cultural position and becomes the rich diverse gift that makes each human unique and special. Every time I experience a moment of this kind I want to share it with everyone. I will my heart to burst wide open and pour the resonance of it into the world. It yearns to take away loneliness, to seep into distressed lives and cause their pain to run away. And everything feels possible because within the very core of that purity, it itself is truth and truth will prevail.

We hugged a lot more, wiped each other's tears of laughter at the question of how to explain this later at the dinner table and finally parted. It made a world of difference to have other human companions too in this adventure the elements had decided to now embark on.

After another three considerably less eventful sessions I was grateful to fall into the familiar routine of tidying and cleaning the room. It was increasingly like living two lives and keeping a foot in each one was ever more challenging. They were like two canoes drifting sideways in different directions. I had a foot in each and eventually I would have to choose or I would have to find a way for the two to find a way to journey together. The problem was, the more I stepped into the worlds of energy, the more of its truth I was given and 21st century living really did not treat energy well, or consider it widely in real ways. Also being with the nature elementals seemed totally natural and comfortable and normal to me, beyond even how I would have anticipated it to feel. It felt like a really enigmatic connection which I was really curious about. Very soon that curiosity would be answered too.

Ordering the room had reorganized the last of my stray thoughts, so ready to drive, I headed to fetch my coat. A strange tugging at my trouser legs stopped me. I looked down to see an assortment of tiny svelte nature spirits looking back at me. They were fine, slender, delicate sylph-like beings with wide, innocent eyes. Carefully and slowly I knelt down before them, knowing instinctively what they had come to do. For the next five minutes they absorbed every one of my senses in a perfect aura cleanse. As they worked I realised they too gave this cleansing service during sleep.

I vowed to remember each morning to thank these realms and closed my eyes sending them waves of thanks and gladness for their being. Word was definitely spreading fast in the nature spirit world that they had human friends close by. Our lives were becoming intrinsically entwined and that trust and closeness would be vital ahead. There was, as the boss had said, a lot of work to do. I wonder how many times he had shouted *that* in my ear!?

Chapter 6

The Water Spirits' Rebirth

Water – The Undine Rhapsody

I am the ripple, the stream, the river, the waves, I, the flow of water, I cause and create how it behaves,

I am calm, I am tempestuous, I am meek and I am strong,

To water I am its life, its spirit. Where water lives I too belong.

I can kiss your skin, balm your mind, calm you with my sway,

or I can hurl you; shake you with my power. I am peace. I am affray. From shallow stream to narrow brook, to the ocean's widest girth, each droplet of my being sustains life and nature's birth.

In ancient times my springs were revered, my source and wells were dressed,

with flower petals, seeds and grains, my virtue baptized and blessed,

And today undines of the underground stream have captured a life with senses awake, too long has the path of the ancients waited to be walked for nature's sake.

Gently the undine beckons, the lure of the mermaids and sirens call, the body and life of water, into its hypnotic gaze I fall,

the undines will guide a life, long have they waited for one to tell,

of ancient truths and sacred sites, willingly I fall under their spell.

And now the undine rhapsody is luring me with its harmony and beauty, Ancient footprints guide, memories of old compel me to their duty, Reverence must be wakened, we are pilgrims rescuing from loss,

The hidden truths and mysteries upon the sacred isle of Samos. With a wave, a flip, a dive, a whirl,

I and the undines stretch, spin, unfurl,

Then, still, I feel how nature holds water in loving thanks,

For when water spirits carry you, all of Earth joins in the dance.

***

It was like plunging into icy water as I left the baking sun light and descended the dark worn stone steps to the cave that lay below the nunnery. Tiny electric shocks of energy began to trill throughout my whole even before I reached the bottom and I slowed to allow my eyes to adjust to the dimly lit gloom. High on a mountain in Pythagoria on the island of Samos stood an ancient holy site where now, remote and devout, the nuns lived out their lives of service and devotion.

And deep below the dense old stone walls of the nunnery and the echoes of the muffled movements of shuffling feet and voices raised in prayer, lay a tiny chapel within a cave.

The cave was more spacious than anticipated, even with the handful of tourists peering around, stepping gingerly on the smooth dank stone floor as they explored every corner. Along the wall facing me a huge deep stone bath sat, its cavernous interior only filled with a pool of shadows now. 'Baptisms? Here? Why down here of all places?'

I turned to comment to Taeke but he was still over on the steps peering at something. It didn't feel right to shout to him, it didn't feel right to be there at all in fact. As that thought entered my head everyone else began to move to the exit. Should I go? But the tiny chapel was drawing me closer. I knew this feeling of compulsion well. When my aura felt like it was cascading with tiny flecks of iron filings being magnetically drawn towards a place, a time, a life hungry for healing light, ravenous for recognition, to be seen and known.

However intense the attraction was, I still stopped at the chapel's open door. Its exterior walls were alive with the flickering lights of tiny candles set amidst a beautiful votive candelabra. 'Someone tends this space, respects this place.' I lit a candle in thanks to them and the intention was magnified by another's intense desire to express their gratitude. What lay within the chapel? I stepped over the threshold.

My eyes adjusted at the same speed as the dull ache in my womb and belly increased to a gnawing bellow of agony. The sheer gut-wrenching loneliness tore at every sinew of humanity and compassion within me. Arms clenched tight around myself and tears springing from my eyes, energy poured through me towards the source of desperation.

"I know you are here, I know." The words were whispered over and over but they broke the silence of hundreds of years. To the recipient, even my whispers were bellowing shouts. For ears that have had no words spoken for them, to them, for centuries, each syllable was a crisp cool raindrop falling onto parched earth. I had never appreciated how painful it must be for a part of Earth to be so numbed by the dry desolation of barren desert land and then to be awakened suddenly by immense drops of rain landing, splashing, spreading, before disappearing abruptly into the parched ground below. In those moments I realised how painful the sheer relief of those first raindrops burrowing themselves into the thirsty Earth are. In those moments of loving energy pouring into the cavernous hole of loneliness, we both hurt, but something held us visually together in the place of knowing that relief can hurt. The remedy itself cannot change the very truth that it will hurt.

With pain aborting and the trilling energy setting to a smooth high-pitched note, I relaxed my arms and dabbed my eyes. Communication through thought vibrations continued to pass but they were of some level or frequency where spoken words do not belong. I had no verbal language. I could now see a fine iridescent shape illuminated against the back wall of the chapel where the worn slab of the altar was set. I was standing facing a simple place to kneel and pray and beyond it a man stood, a man who looked as ancient and weathered as the stone he had lived amidst. There was no distinction between where the brilliant sequins of wisdom he was and the wisdom and intelligence of the ancient mountain rock began. It was as if the lives had combined, entwined, become all one. Just as the cave, the chapel, the mountain echoed with a collective wisdom, so too did this life resonate like a tuning fork aligned to their vibration. How had he become so attuned, so in sympathy, with the elements and form of this island? And how could he have left, when he departed the physical life, when it and him were so imbued?

An alcove in the wall next to me caught my eye. Placed with obvious sentiment, numerous gem stones shone, brightening the gloomy indent. One crystal sparkled, beckoned. Like a child I reached out my hand to touch it and behind me the energy leapt and shrank back. Shocked at my own insensitivity I swung round. Just a few gems and candles held the only energy of connection this life had to any semblance of recognition or thought for it and I had forgotten my manners entirely at the sight of a shiny rock. "I am so, so sorry, that was insensitive of me." I spoke quietly, directly to him, and waited. The mass of energy settled. It moved closer. Then it swelled and enveloped me.

There are many times in your life, when in service or deep reflection, you are so filled with the grace of fine energy responding, that a profound sense of peace settles every cell of your being. For those troubled by the culture's inhumanity and ever widening social divides, these moments recalibrate the soul, spirit and life within, knowing that however painful and lonely the mission may feel at times, the place where all is in harmony and at one in purpose is eternal and ever close by. You emerge from those reconnections refreshed in the knowing you are not born a long way from home after all. Just like the snail, we travel life always within our home, yet when we manifest into occupying a physical form that outer and inner shell of matter makes us feel distinct, separated, singular. But to a snail its sense of self is shell, home, earth all united. And when we touch that unity again we become rewired to the integral truth we are a sequin of.

Time stood still as I experienced a melting into a pure oneness of welcome and expansive peace and as I emerged from the mutually grateful energetic embrace and we become two distinct beings again. I knew I had been loaded like a microchip with intelligence and I was about to be led on a mission that was to be my deepest honour yet. The deep sense of mutual knowing and togetherness bound us in a profound way. No longer did loneliness fill the chapel. Instead a powerful serenity hung tangibly in the air. Bowing deeply, I said, "I will return," and gently backed out of the chapel.

At that moment the invisible barrier that had kept the cave devoid of visitors the whole time broke and two ladies, heads covered respectfully, stepped carefully from the last stair. Their eyes adjusted, fell on the chapel and they headed straight for the open door. I watched, interested to see if the strong atmosphere would be noticed. They had barely stepped over the threshold before their eyes met knowingly and with voices respectfully low they spoke together of the powerful presence and peace the chapel held. Energy and the law of attraction. When a heightened vibration pitches its signal those who can receive it will be more in sympathy and attunement with it. Glad of courteous visitors to warm the wise man's resonance, I hurried up the steps, the sense of mission more urgent and eager than it had ever felt.

The contrast of brightness and space and a wall of heat hit me as I emerged and ran over to Taeke. "A lot happened in there, that's why I've been so long. There is something important to do and I need to do some research of the land right away."

Armed with numerous maps we returned to the apartment where I began to study the mountain and town of Pythagoria. The mystic and magic of the mountain and the beliefs held still in the native islanders of the elemental beings was obvious to see. Pythagorus had spent much time high in a cave atop the mountain deep in contemplation and discovery, communing with the ancient wisdoms of the land. And stories abounded of a mysterious light that would be seen at night at certain times of the year emanating from Pythagorus's mountain top cave.

But it was the sheer number of streams running into and through Pythagoria that stood out.

The maps were peppered with endless tiny blue lines and they all conveyed and ran through the point where the nunnery stood. Over one, close to it, a bridge had been marked in tiny print. I leaned in closer to read the name 'Fairies Bridge'.

"It's sacred water, Taeke," I announced. "There is something important the holy man needs doing for the water spirit energies I am sure. It seems that every stream and waterway meet under that nunnery." Taeke looked at me nonplussed, "Did you not see the stream running through the cave?" I leaned back from the map with a look of frustration, "Clearly *not*! As usual I appear to have taken the long route in! Where is it?"

"Before the last few steps, another set of really old rough steps lead off down to the stream where it flows in and through and then beyond. It was lit with tiny lights, so the nuns still keep that part maintained. I went off to look at that but you went straight in." "Yeah, I did because I was fixed on that huge bath for baptism and wondering why such a massive article had been built in a cave."

Things were clicking into place in parts of me that always worked in such a sensory way that the feelings led to the thoughts to the intuitive knowings. It was a curious kind of unfolding of reality where, as the jigsaw pieces got slotted into place, you knew something within was holding the picture. However it certainly wasn't a part of the brain dedicated to many thought processes as it too also seemed to become conscious of the picture appearing only when it was voiced, a very different thing to following a train of thoughts, "The nuns might maintain it, but it's tradition, service, and I don't think this is enough for whatever is reaching out here. And they, and the holy man, are within the confines of the nunnery walls. Something is needed beyond those walls and a different connection to what the nuns bring in their collective devotions."

Without hesitation it was decided that Taeke would drop me off in the town early the next morning and leave me there for the day. I knew I would be led and accompanied, but I could not have envisaged how important the pilgrimage was for so many. In fact it later made me realise why the paths of pilgrims were trodden so devotedly, their ley lines powering the planets' energy through their systems and guiding them like a sat nav to nature's own sacred sites. Many of those power points upon earth, are now marked by ancient churches and cathedrals, built much later by hands skilled in sacred geometry, so that by design the finest energies would be captured and directed according to human will.

"Where are you going first?" Taeke asked as he dropped me at the centre of the town. I just raised my eyebrows and smiled. They knew, my system knew and I would be let in on the mission details as we went. Looking left and right my feet instantly chose right and set off at a steady pace.

They seemed propelled by a drawing, magnetic energy that not only compelled my feet to steadily stride under its spell but, like iron filings in unanimous attraction, the inner lives too felt in peace and harmony with each passing moment. And so it was, led as if by the Pied Piper himself, on and on we walked, in unity with ever increasing effervescent radiance. I had become lost in the fascination of simply observing my own inner state in communion with Earth energies, the very fabric of each intricate aspect of itself, when my feet abruptly stopped.

"What do you sense?" The tone of the voice was gentle, knowing, the impression was that of a teacher enjoying both student and lesson. Moisture filled my mouth. "Water! Below us runs an underground stream." My words seemed to be carried by airwaves that danced. It was as if myriads of eager minds were capturing their resonance and echoing them, transmitting their vibration for miles around. The moment stretched as if time itself was under a spell cast by the flowing currents of air and water in a sacred dance with Earth.

Then my feet joined in and our route undulated and wove, curving up embankments and back down again, halting at points where more streams below us flowed in. Each water course was acknowledged, thanked, revered and the vibration of those words and thoughts carried like the stars in a children's story book spiraling from Merlin's wand. Even water itself felt thirsty for those words of gratitude, for the very ceremony itself.

Eventually my legs carried me up a sloping embankment which sheltered an ancient burial site that had been dug deep within it. From my position above I could see it had long been excavated so all that remained were the many deep cut holes of varying sizes. Holes cut to the size of their previous occupants. Tailor made as their final resting places. Now devoid of those intended to be at rest, at peace. Just empty shells, the discarded husks left after the treasure had been pirated away.

The feet of many curious sightseers had worn a path into and through the site and I was about to follow it when I abruptly stopped myself. It felt so intrusive to take another step, to even look for another second. I turned away, sad, dismayed. What gave anyone the right to dig the earth from around bodies at peace for centuries? To move them from their final resting place?

How did that affect the energy of the land and the resonance, the continuance, of the lives lived?

"Step gently on this Earth," my mind repeated as I walked over to sit on a large rock and observe the site from there. As the clear focus of intention formed in me to bring healing to the land, force powered through me. The pitch of the atmosphere rang in my ears, climbing, increasing, until all I could hear was the pure whistle of potent remedy coursing laser like through the top of my head. It powered out through my eyes, poured from my hands, my feet, deep into the ground, spreading like tree roots into every corner of each life connected to them, joining them all in a sacred embrace of peace, of settlement. If the amount of energy could have been replicated in physical mass the gaping ugly gash the excavations had scarred the Earth with would have been filled and once again invisible to the eye. Something had long waited for a conduit to channel healing settlement here.

I held the focus until the force had gradually ebbed and ceased. Time no longer existed in the realm now occupied. Past present, future, all a reality together. Every microcosm and cell within nature, within life, interconnected, joined.

Me, a part of the whole, but it, the whole of me and beyond. As I sat on the rock breathing in the enhanced atmosphere and enjoying the feeling of no separation, the sensations of no limits, no skin, no layers dividing what I am from all else, a butterfly flew past my face. Its flight path was only centimeters from me and, because of the acutely instinctive space I was in, its journey past appeared to happen in ultra-slow motion.

Fine gossamer wings stirring a delicate breeze, tiny antennae and a vivid feast of colours, a fiesta for the eyes, brushed past the end of my nose. But the visual clarity was secondary to the audible awareness that arose as she flew pass. 'Follow me.' The message she carried was crystal clear and my feet did not need telling twice.

Being led by a butterfly is a rare and delightful experience. The urge to pirouette, to dip, to surge, to dance in the trace of its flight is only quelled by the reality of the lack of dexterity. So I did the best job I could, following her beyond the burial mound, over another embankment and down into a dip where the butterfly hovered and spun, then flew along some more and repeated her moves again.

At each exact point she hovered, lay old rusted metal covers. She had brought me to the ancient wells where islanders of old had drawn pure water from the underground springs. Did a butterfly once lead them to the source or was it their uncluttered senses that felt the presence of moisture?

Senses that were bright and free of the signals of radio waves, Wi-Fi, pylons to confuse and coarsen. The butterfly carried the reverence helped by all the island life for the ancient peoples and their sensitivity of celebrations and thanks. They and the islands were one ...it sustained them, and they thus revered and respected it. On behalf of both deep reconnections were being re-awakened and rejoiced in.

Transmitting deep 'Thanks to all' and blowing the butterfly a kiss, I made my way back past the burial site and continued the winding journey the many streams formed. Sometimes my feet would march me down a path to stand me in front of a tree and a communication would occur. A transmission between the tree and whatever/whoever was also accompanying thus passed, then onwards again we would go. It was fascinating to be the willing vehicle through which much could be conveyed, reconnect and travel.

Eventually the 'vehicle' needed a refueling stop and my feet gladly pulled towards a taverna with the most magical garden at the rear. Choosing a table tucked in a charming corner, I ordered and took out my notebook to write. I had been so absorbed in starting to process through the morning's journey that I was not conscious of the garden emptying of people. It was only as I thanked the lady as she delivered the delicious Greek salad and chilled wine that I realized I was yet again the only soul occupying the space.

The pen flew across the pages as insights, descriptions of subtle aspects of the experiences moved into my consciousness as I wrote. The atmosphere became charged, electrified as the ancient connections and simple delight at nature's sustaining elements found an anchor and further expression in me. My skin felt soft like plump velvet rose petals in their fullness and prime. And my aura felt like a glass filled with Prosecco the effervescence impossible to contain as it fizzed and overflowed the purifying energies, transmitting truth into land that had long awaited being awoken by that once familiar vibration. The garden remained empty of people but the atmosphere filled, the pages filled, on and on it went in such a way.

Then my hand hesitated and my gaze shifted up from the page. It met a row of tiny beady eyes staring, heads cocked, inquisitively at me. Along each edge of the table just inches from me, perched rows of tiny birds. Keeping my movements slow I glanced around. Next to me the tree was draped, the wall was a mass and even the back of the chair in which I sat was covered with tiny birds. It was as if the whole of nature had been awoken by the silver kiss of the energy and now, I was in the midst of a Disney scene direct from 'Snow White'.

Both birds and human alike were captivated by the chance to share the precious peace and closeness that is so meant and intended to be. We remained together, a tableau of sacred space, through which all upon the island could connect. Pure crystal rain drops of force nourishing a long-parched land. Elementals of land, air, fire and water drinking in the sustenance of again being known, being close to human kind.

Thought waves of thanks and of farewells began to pass through me. The communion was drawing to a close. My gaze swept slowly across all the places the birds sat, intent to acknowledge every set of eyes present, each little pulsing life within felt more precious, special and unique than I had ever realized before. Then they rose, en masse and seconds later the door from the Taverna creaked open and tourists once again trickled into the garden. Glancing at my phone, I realized that over an hour had passed yet not one soul had come into the garden in that whole time, just like the cave.

Taking as many mental snap shots of the garden as possible, I paid and left. Now my feet took me back in the direction of town and the nunnery high above. The winding waterways below formed a natural flow to follow and every cell and sinew of my being felt totally in harmony and unity with all else that walked with us.

As we began to climb the mountain road toward the nunnery every sound of nature was echoing through me with a clarity and frequency I had not known before. It was as though I could understand the language of nature in every form and even the creaking of branches of trees as I passed them, were bowing and speaking their welcome as I ascended to the Holy site. As I reached a wall, just below the entrance to the nunnery church my feet halted and I looked down, welcoming its accommodating height after the long climb.

Outside the church many smartly dressed people were gathering, exchanging welcomes and hugs. Suddenly I heard the familiar notes of English voices amongst them and I watched fascinated as a gentleman gathered the large crowds together, a baby in a christening gown held proudly in his arms.

Although laced with a distinct Greek accent, his English was perfect and his voice carried perfectly to me as he began to explain, to what was clearly his English wife's family, the importance of the church and the Holy Site for baptisms. My focus wanted to flip and ask how they could orchestrate the timing of this so perfectly, but I forgot all stray thoughts and seized the moment to the full.

For the proud father the importance of his child being christened in this place could not be overstated. He explained with great emphasis and expression about the wise Holy man who had centuries before lived his life in religious solitude in the cave below. The Holy man was known for his incredible wisdom and connection to the island, knowledge and devout faith, and how many people for decades had come to speak to the Holy man to seek out his counsel and advice.

The waters here known as Holy and spirited and through their purification ceremonially birthed, cleansed a life to live well, to live truly and decently.

Hundreds of baptisms had been performed inside of his cave cathedral from his tiny chapel. The respect and reverence for him, for this place reached far and wide and had endured over the years. So thus, the nuns still tended the chapel and the waters, keeping safe the memory and tradition to facilitate the many families that still live close and travel to this church to bless their children with the best possible baptism and start in life they could have.

At these many mysteriously synchronized times you yet again deepen in the trust that all life is an interconnected weave of millions of threads. Amidst that giant intricate pattern we all exist, making choices, living our lives, being drawn and compelled by invisible threads that stretch like nerve endings emitting pulses, signals and hauntings through our sensory systems to guide us to our purpose and destiny. The visual picture is like a cobweb and just like the spider positions itself at the centre of the web where it can feel every vibration that both elements of wind and water and physical life cause as they enter that domain; so too sits the core, pulsing origin of all Creation.

And that universal place of arising understands and knows all from its sensory headquarters as each section of the web has energy life forms and intelligences who receive and transmit work in service as part of the whole, just as our own nerve pathways do too.

Becoming human means aspects of that whole must move inside of a physical vehicle of their own, a form that is microcosmic replica of that intricate web and intelligent design. The human form is an extraordinary masterpiece through which the universal source can experience itself, discover what it is unto itself.

But that means to do so the source must gift a part of itself into each human, the spirit, the universal guide, an inner homing signal, for the host wills that all find their way back home, thus true love has no ownership. It gifts that part of itself freely and waits, listens, watches, learns through it and hopes, yearns for its safe return. That part of each of us is like the chick leaving the nest and just like a parent, Creation's core sends us all the help and sign posts it to assist each to succeed, to fulfil the life purpose intended.

Everything else within the Spider web faces inwards towards the centre, however we stand on the peripheries of the fabric of the web, and we face out. For Planet Earth to evolve and to manifest the elements into physical forms she must be maintained whilst spinning in a unique and rare space which means we too orbit in an ecology, an environment that is remote in its form. Inside of the experience, beauty and rarity Nature and Mother Earth are, our human task is to refine our connections to climb the silver threads to our destiny, to unlock our life's calling. As we learn so too does the Core.

However, the mighty intelligences that caused and willed this into being are cosmic master masons. They knew we could get more disconnected and become lost to the missions sacred purpose. So, the Earth gifts each of us a soul which acts like a planetary sat nav to find our way around. Being human is like being a space man, an astronaut, yet in reverse. Except finding, how to travel and navigate with human systems is far more intricate than a spaceship.

As I watched the families file into the church, I felt further inside of the spider web than ever before. The Christening service was long underway by the time I had considered all those silver threads, the parents, all the lives who had moved into their places only when the time was right, to make the journey and the whole experience possible.

Shakespeare said, "All the world is a stage and upon it we are merely players."

I thanked the Directors, the stage hands, the lighting crew and the whole of the Elemental and Essence Realms and began to make my way back to the apartment. The space was respectively there for the family now. I would return tomorrow.

As I faced the votive candelabra inside of the cave the next day, the quiet words of the Teacher once again spoke to me as it did when I walked back down the hillside the previous day. His words centered and focused me. "You have walked the path of the Ancients, we thank you."

These words barmed confirmation and thanks and chased any noises of disbelief away. My systems knew what to do, somehow, they always do.

I selected four candles, placing them carefully, North, South, East & West. Was it the teacher who had filled my dreams with knowing that I would wake with? Was the teacher the wise Holy man whose energy had enveloped me, claiming my systems as his own, just for a time? Because he knew he could, because my radiation told him he must, its openness allowing him finally all he needed to be at peace, at rest. Just one human system, one devoted human who would travel with the elements was all he needed and waited for.

Because when I awoke that morning, I knew that the ceremony, the reverence within the walk of the Ancients had been within how they lived, breathed and thought. And in their grace of thanks each day for what had sustained them, the elementals of all sources were consciously acknowledged, brought gifts and richly powered as energy beings by the natural and pure relationship they and humans had together. They built bridges for the fairies to cross, they placed flower petals, seeds, herbs and offerings by the wells as thanks, as a return.

The ancients and the elementals walked, flowed and traversed the land together gathering together at ceremonies, joining and being joined. As nature's elements thrived and stayed powered by that mutual way of life the waters become charged, electric, alive and pure.

Each coursing stream carried that energy and continually flowed, ever flowed until the bounty of many streams all converged as one; the one stream that flowed right through the Ancient Cave. The wise hermit had never had to leave the cave because every connection to every rock, plant, tree and life flowed to him. In his quiet devotions and prayers, he offered almost a Holy mass for the elementals themselves in his cave cathedral and the more richly imbued with the energies, senses and truths of the island he became the more people sought the knowledge that lived with him. The island lived and breathed in every form through him and with him. He became its sacred archive, its religious core and he became an intrinsic part of its very being and soul.

Although the charged spirited particles of water were sought after for baptisms for rebirth and for christenings, it however was not originally holy water. Over time, in deep constant states of prayer and meditation the holy man became wise through the knowledge the water carried to him. As he gazed for hours, days, and years into the pure crystal depths with questions with deep human enquiry, he found that profound insights and truths emerged through his systems, trickling, dripping and wending their way into his consciousness. His reverence for the sacred power of the water grew and flourished and his devotion to it too.

I realised why the oracles would often stare into a pool of water. Why water became known as a force of divination for seeing the future and for understanding the present and defining the past. And why it is called a 'Reflective State'.

The love and gratitude within the holy man wanted to share that divine connection and grace lives with purity, with the energy of every form and life of the island. Each new life is welcomed on Earth by the reverent rhapsody of the elements that filled every pool of water that flowed into the cave. Every new life began divinely connected to the land upon which it had been born. And each life that sought counsel, sustenance, belief, faith, inspiration and healing would be confirmed and christened with the waters as a blessing of renewal and rebirth. It felt that it was as much the will of the water itself to facilitate this ceremony as was for him. Together they were in service, for Earth and all higher planes that graced and bestowed its love and bounty. The most profound and moving relationship with the elementals and essences to ever be caused to meet.

I lit the four candles of Earth, Fire, Air and Water and watched the lights flicker around the chapel wall, breathing in a sense of what had replaced the heaviness in the cave.

Staring at the dancing flames I spoke aloud, "Thank you for showing me why aborigines sing the song lines." I could feel him smile and I could feel his energy now full with peace.

He was glad I knew.

The teacher in him had taught me well. And it would again, often, in times ahead. Now he was free, free to move into his next destiny. It had been a long time coming, even for one as devoted as him.

For a while after he passed, the islanders continued to live simply with value and respect with and for the land. However, as relationships with elementals dwindled and people who carried the experiences and connections died, our truths became lost, beliefs became folklore and ceremonies became traditions that held no real sense nor emitted genuine gratitude. Electricity brought the static heat and coarse energy onto the island causing the elemental life to further retreat into isolated places, corners where peace and pure air remained.

Water became piped to houses, became a commodity on tap, so the simple daily ceremonies of plunging a bucket into the wells and drawing the precious pure clear spring water that would be valued and used carefully once it reached home were lost. No more did hands work pumps and marvel at the grace of the substance that enabled food to grow and life to be sustained. Little by little the human and elemental connection dwindled away as machines watered the land, denying lands and human systems their sensory connection to the Earth.

And as the sacred water's life and soul dwindled, so too did the wise Holy man's presence. To leave was impossible. His energy flowed like the life blood of the island's soul and spirit and the more it ebbed away the sadder and lonelier he became. His own destiny beyond was not his first concern and for a long time his presence had still been sought out. But as the seekers dwindled and time passed, his window of chance to leave had passed and so too had his will to do so. For his love of the elementals, the island, he needed to perform one last act of devotion and reawaken the land energies, reconnect them and the Ancients, and cause the waters to again glow with the spirit of the land.

He just needed one life that believed. One human system that was known to the nature spirits, to walk those ancient paths with senses awake and reverence alive. The streams and rivulets that are, and always have been, the song lines of the island.

Through human feet Earth receives our thanks, the vibrations of gratitude drawn down deep from our auras. The aborigines know the songs of the soul of the earth upon which they live. They sing to replenish, rejuvenate, recalibrate themselves and the land.

To restore the connections and to be with Earth in harmony as we are intended to be. "I bet you know the songs of Samos too," I said.

The candle flames burned high and the waters' rippling reflections now stretched into the spaces creating mirrors from the shiny stones in the cave walls.

"This whole cave is an oracle, isn't it?" Every facet of its being throughout must have been alight with reflections and the more powered it became the more every single stone became able to reveal the land's history locked within it. And every stone has a unique story to tell of Earth's evolution and of humans' past.

I had never expected to be shown more. Already I had been gifted an experience, allowed to perform an honourable task, but the generosity of Earth and creation is limitless, and the cave was at last once again alive.

There was no need to enter the chapel as I knew it was time for the teacher to finally leave and the cave was signaling its thanks and farewells. We all knew we would be connected. And student and teacher would always remember, always be glad. I promised to light a candle for the elementals every day and walked away.

As I arrived back home a few days later the first thing I saw was a parcel addressed to me. It was heavy and bulky. Inside was a box with a note taped to the top which said, "I saw this and felt it was right for you, Love, Ali."

What weighty item had my soul sister sent me? The box lid surrendered and inside sat a large salt lamp with a tea light buried deep in its core.

"If you elementals can influence from Samos to Ali in Birmingham you have seriously got your power back," I laughed. "I fully intend you to keep it too," I confirmed. And the candle deep in the salt lamp cave was duly lit!

Chapter 7

Fire – The Fire Spirit Ignites

I am the tender warmth in the glowing log, in the flame that flickers and flares,

I am the bubbling of the sulphur spring, the reflection of sunlight as it glares,

And bounces lights and colours from the raindrops' pure vibrant cascade,

As fiery sunbeams and water meet and rainbow's beauty is displayed.

Do you fear me or revere me as I sparkle, crackle and ignite? Do I repel you and alarm you or are you attracted to my light?

Are you a fluttering moth drawn to my flame or a deer fleeing forest fire in fright? Do I mesmerize, hypnotize and allure you? Or do I petrify you with my might?

I am cleaner, redeemer, creator, destroyer, Eternally the wheel of life turns,

I begin, I cause, I power, I destruct. I'm the spirit within you that burns,

To unlock your destiny, unleash your power, I am the spark the universe bestows.

Wake up! LIVE! Let the spirit ignite

In its radiance your soul richly grows.

I can travel in the dragons from

the east, west, north and south.

Consume, transmute lower energies,

flames leaping from my mouth.

I can travel in the dragon to places finer forces cannot go.

And purify the coarseness with my blazing scarlet glow.

Summon NOT the dragon unless your mission is crystal clear,

He is a Knight of Purpose. A warrior without fear,

For the winged warrior goes where the Angels fear to tread, In the service of its purpose fire will light the dragon's breath. From East to West, North to South the fire elementals surge,

The eternal wheel of life where beginnings and endings merge.

***

It is very true when it is said that the more you get to know, the less you realize you really do know! What I really 'knew' about the myriad of nature elementals would fit on a postage stamp, but the simple effervescent sense of them and their delightful childlike honesty was becoming a frequent and familiar radiation.

However, I was about to discover how clearly they influence and cause the character of each landmass and country, and just how powerful and strong that personality can be. The nature spirits had also decided that it was timely to introduce me to the reality that when you meet a fire spirit there is absolutely nothing subtle about it at all.

And as usual in this harmonious and delightful working relationship they had decided to give me no advance warnings at all! I guess sometimes the entertainment value is more important and carefully planned for too.

In between the weeks being increasingly packed with therapy clients, I was also getting busy with the ecology work which took many forms. One week I would be building a colour exhibition, the next cleaning a home or business premises and then following that with work in a school and university. The variety was great and with every new departure and request the learning piled in and the experiences mounted up.

I had been asked by a fellow therapist to design a therapy room. His practice however is in acupuncture and very attuned to it he is too. Despite the foundational aspects of natural light and material being a given for any therapy space, designing one would be attractive to Eastern energies and enable them to manifest and bring their healing powers and wisdom to bear was proving to be a fascinating task. From the start I knew that loading my own healing ecologies into the space was neither going to be fitting nor respecting the amazing ancient sources of wisdom and power the Eastern healing modalities hold.

Within two days of visualization with the space I was finding there was nothing gentle or understated about the Chinese forces at all. They built that Great Wall not to keep people out, but to keep mighty forces contained. So before there would be any connections made and knowledge down loaded to me I had to find a way over, under or through that wall!

So I worked the only way I knew how with persistence, constancy and respect. Placing myself within the space time and time again visually asking them what forms, materials, shapes, colours and patterns suited and enhanced them, until shapes and dimensions began to form and appear on the paper before me. Weight and depth, everything had great substance and presence. The precision was not the cool, detached, clean lined minimalism that Japanese frequencies bring in silently and modestly. This had embellishment and arrived with a resounding statement.

As each piece of furniture, art, material, pattern and shape slotted itself into its chosen position and placement it would fly through my faculties and pencil wielding hand like a warrior kicking down the door then placing his two feet squarely in the space he had thus claimed. Then, arms folded out in front of his chest the warrior would take the form of what belonged in that position and was required for the precision and skill Chinese Medicine holds and issues.

As much as I resisted the classic visuals of the red and gold and strove for the space to be created by them, I could see clearly why the most magnetic, physical of colours and the most weighty metal of all was so indicative of China.

After a week I became accustomed to the long periods of petition and nothingness, which was then blasted through like a juggernaut driving through the visual space in my mind. This had become so familiar I no longer was gripping the chair in slightly nervous anticipation of the responses of these mighty forces. I had always held a huge respect and fascination for Chinese medicine as regularly and often the Ancients' healing knowledge of the body systems would surface during healing sessions as I worked with colour and kinesiology methods. Later I would check out the information and insights a client's system had revealed to me against Chinese understandings of the organs, systems and energy flow of the human form and always they would be exactly the same. Without fail I could find I had organically rediscovered what the Chinese already knew 5000 years ago! The template of the workings of the human form physically and energetically is a perfect foundation of truth that holds intact today as it did those myriads of years ago.

These great minds however were graced by mighty forces that are unsubtle and lack finesse in form, because when they are connected into the fertile faculties of those Ancient doctors and seekers of the truth and purpose, the intricate details and finite diagrams that were produced take your breath away. An enduring record of the incredible knowledge and invaluable reference points, always.

Finally, every detail was drawn, every material was listed and the design was ready. At that point I had no inkling of how much they had enjoyed designing their own space in which to manifest. All I knew was, that what was on paper had not come from memory banks in the corners of my own mind, it was as intended of them and for them and the integrity of my working ethos remained intact. And when I handed over the completed drawing and detailed descriptions a fortnight later the satisfaction was mutual amidst all parties.

The challenge had been thoroughly enjoyable with lots of new senses and experiences and as always, many parts within wanted to stay with it further and explore deeper. But there were clients aplenty booked, and land healing work. The need is to try to be entirely with the present and what occupies that moment. So, I had to pull myself together to focus all within and be present to the needs and responses that came through each day.

It was the end of a busy weekend of therapies and the treatment room needed an extra thorough physical and energetic cleanse. I threw open the window (air), poured steaming hot water into a bowl (water) and began to scrub the room (earth). The cleansing, purifying smoke of the incense, the fire element, would come last. Only when the space was physically fit.

The very best and most faithful friends in all the world a human life has are the fine universal essences and Earth's elemental realms and no healing work can be performed without them. However, they cannot enter into an unkempt or unclean ecology without its adversely affecting them and just as I would not invite my family and friends to stay in a dirty bedroom, on principle I would not petition energy companions to do so either. So however late the hour, the room would be cleaned and purified and tonight it was late, very late indeed.

I was weary but intent on cleaning with a willingness to fill the atmosphere with clear thoughts, so a thorough job was ensured. Once into the task, with music accompanying, it felt, as ever assisted by many ethereal feather dusters and one hour later I felt content with the result. A final rub to a smear on the beautiful stained glass window in one corner, an extra polish to the taps in another, a considered tweak to the chairs in the opposite corner and one last sweep of the clean, crisp white cotton on the couch and all was ready for the incense to complete the cleanse and settle the energy to rest with mindful thanks.

The thought had barely surfaced when a commanding voice drowned it totally out. "Go and stand and face the stained glass window. NOW!"

I hot tailed it into that corner, faced the window and gripped the surround for good measure. "What the heck was this all about now?!"

Energetically the sound was the loudest roar I have ever heard. The sheer speed and power that propelled itself through the room was enormous. It was not frightening. Just completely awe inspiring. The size, the potency, driving source of such energy and force of such magnitude is a little like standing in a room with a Boeing 757 jet engine running. It was in and through and gone in seconds, but I was still gripping the window surround minutes later too stunned to even attempt to move. Even my breath seemed to barely dare to disturb the highly charged energy left in the room. When my fingers began to peel themselves free it felt like warm loving arms were gently holding my shoulders and patiently turning me around. Waves of calm rippled through me, reassuring vibrations reached deep into my being. "Thank you," I finally managed, "Thank you so much for making sure I was safe."

The room felt so energetically clean I was sure that NASA would see it reflected on the moon! "But what the heck was that?" I wished I could see the wide smile on the Guardian that night as he replied. "That my love was a FIRE DRAGON, He came from the East to thank you."

A lump of emotion formed in my throat as I tried to process just how abundantly generous nature's forces are. "Wow," I finally managed lamely. "I guess their therapy room really is right for them. So grateful and glad to know." "You did well. Really well," he replied, "and now go home, you have earned your rest."

Perhaps the Fire Dragon knew what lay in store ahead. Maybe as always they knew that I had to meet every elemental force and they me, within a time frame for their master plan to help.

And in true style they chose a way that brought the gratitude of the Eastern energies and filled me further with a reverence for their magnitude and power.

Whatever the truth it was a very good job I managed to slip through a gap in that Great Wall. Because I and my systems would need to hold no fear of powerful forces ahead. And we would yet again be helped by a mighty fire spirit in a task that involved every form of elemental being. But this time I would be helping them. I would be healing the fire spirits themselves by finally extinguishing a fire that had ruthlessly killed a settlement of innocent men, women and children hundreds of years before. A blaze created by the hand of soldiers who had used fire in their own destructive way. Traumatizing the land for miles around and locking that memory shock deep within it. So deep, it still raged red hot today, emitting ethereal smoke signals of despair to any eyes that it could find that could see.

A whole village of people still held in the echo of that time, searching for their loved ones, unable to leave. One lady and child united but a whole settlement still to heal and an army stretching across the horizon remorseful, begging with their eyes for the endless replay of the suffering they had caused. The time had come to meet the past. A past filled with fire spirits who only knew destruction and were running free.

Chapter 8

Battling the Inferno
of the Past

Part 1

Summon not the dragon unless your mission is pure in heart and mind. Use NOT the Fire spirit energy to harm your fellow human kind.

For if we take this fire as our weapon and unleash its mighty source.

The centuries will pass before nature can rebalance that destructive force.

I, Fire, – can burn as flames that sear, lick, ever ravenous, consuming.

Or within seeping bubbling lava from volcano's mouth I spill, molten fuming. Burping, steaming, and fizzing within creating nature's spa.

Or perhaps I'll light your rescue beacon to be seen from land afar.

I, Fire, – within the very sparks of energy that drive your heart and nerves. The vitamin within your thoughts whether kind, informed or clear.

Both causer and destroyer but I fire cannot choose the master I serve. Never take me away from Creation's purpose, it's really not a good idea.

Do, I fire spirit warn you, do I remind you strong and clear? That we the mighty elements are the controlling forces here.

Nature's balance is the life blood through which we unite and breathe And only late in our destiny to humans we did bequeath.

Freedom to live and enjoy our sacred earth's rare and beautiful space. Time now to realign, to remember the humans' true respectful place.

When you refine the human purpose and are aligned within. So too will you caretake and love all your kith and kin.

And with gentle minds and caring hearts the energies of nature will all restore. We await your awakening with eagerness..... hurry, hurry we implore.

***

The past had claimed the whole of our sensory systems at the outset, so it pulled us back to its wounds and torment the moment we resumed our focus. Boundaries and buildings faded out of sight, replaced by the scene of the settlement all around us stretching over the fields at either side. Beyond, instead of the clean welcome lines of grass, rock and tree scape, the horizon was filled with hundreds of soldiers, waiting, watching. Their purgatory, to watch the replay of the death and destruction wrought by their hands.

Guilt and dismay poured from their desperate souls, willing it to stop, to end. But the credits couldn't roll until the gully of misery and bloodshed stopped, until the screaming anguish of the shock was quietened and healed.

We came to cleanse a house occupying a modest size patch of land and now we stood visually and audibly in the midst of a vast expanse of carnage. Our eyes snapped open, we had seen enough. "We work from the front," I said firmly. "You stand where the ground was first disturbed with the digging, I need to stand farther back." My mind was being pulled to the river which flowed through the valley below.

We both knew how to hold a healing space, to follow the visual pictures and the audible directives. Neither of us feared being moved like chess pieces mentally and physically as whatever master plan unfolded through the circuitries of the senses, it required us to do its work. Never before though had our minds been called upon to hold a space this vast. And never one so long trapped by such misery and suffering created by human hands.

As we took our positions all we both knew implicitly was that the healing realms would never ask of us more than we could handle. My arm again throbbed with the recall of the searing burns. Heart pounded with the sounds of fear and the smell of savage blazing infernos, death all around. And then through a chink of bright light opening up, I saw again the joyful relief of the mother running to scoop into her arms the daughter who had long before moved into the safety of beyond. I inhaled the deep sense of healing peace and with each breath surrendered the whole of myself to the healing realms. The centre of my forehead pulsed. My mind stretched, open wide. The atmosphere whined, trilled, rang, filling my head with its sound.

Long, oh so very long had the land waited to be taken out of that time. The elements stirred and in unison rose all around me. The spirits of air, whirring, powering in from every direction.

Then the body of the river, surging, releasing its very essence. On mass the elementals, urgent, rushing, cascading in. At last, at last they could respond, could finally end the trauma that had pained them to their core. Visually my mind was razor sharp to every detail spanning 360 degrees for miles around. Through it every realm communicated, watched, directed. I had become a human periscope, a main frame computer through which all information, detail, command and feedback could pass.

Nature's elementals moved in like an orchestra ... first the wind section... notes of a symphony coming from afar, the reedy sounds of clarinets, a hint of a tin whistle. The air stirred around me, penetrated sharply, bristled into my ears, "Hold your mind firm." It was an order not a request. "I will," the reply was the chorus from the choir of the many who stood with and within me. Bugles, trumpets, trombones, big brass. The orchestra's wind section approached from every direction, the balance and synchronicity of every part of the score allowing each facet to be heard. A battalion of elementals whirring closer, faster from far and near.

The wind whirled, unfurled itself through me. "When we bring the waters, take its power deep into the ground. Contain the fire at all costs and keep us all safe." I felt my mind intensify, I saw it draw down a vast shield and surround the area with a wall of force. My head ached and throbbed with the piercing whistle of laser like energy boring through it. "This ends today. With peace there will be no more harm."

The intense protection of maternal and paternal realms held my body strongly, powerfully. The 'Will' within mind and heart like a column of granite. I knew nothing would break me, could break me, for what had hard wired itself through me was too vast, too permanent to allow anything but it's Will to succeed.

The first draft of immense elementals hovered high like mighty tornadoes across the spread of the land. Their task, to cool the atmosphere degree by careful degree and starve the fire of oxygen, its fuel. Upon each one guardians hold their gaze, directing them, causing them to retreat, to cool, intensely watchful of their safety.

Behind me, a distance away, I felt the very life of the river surge. A large part of the wind section I knew was approaching from that direction, whipping up the power and presence of the water spirits into their midst. Not a trickle, a rivulet or a stream of water elementals this, but a legion, a torrent of pure fire consuming power. The very vitamin of waters saturating being now swept into the swirling air currents, the very life of water now carried, like a babe in arms by the mighty power of air. As the water spirits joined the concert my head filled with the sounds of the string section striking up en masse. This was not a coarse mechanical battle strategy. I was at the centre of a harmonious symphony. A breath-taking melody of team work that only nature in all her glory can summon and perform.

My respect, reverence and pride for Mother Earth ignited to another level as each battalion of combined air and water forces moved across the expanse of the land. My mind, every sinew and faculty within me, sent the mighty flame drenching energy deeper and deeper into the bowels of the earth, forcing the water energy to penetrate further and further. Every corner, space, square inch of the land mass flooding with the welcome drench of cool saturation. The steely focus emitting through my mind made me shake with its power as it forced the waters' energy to penetrate ever deeper to the core of the inferno, to the raging red angry centre of the blaze.

I was aware of numerous instructions firing through me telling the frontline elementals each time to withdraw, peel away in formations and hurry to the cool of the river's banks to safety, to restore, to recharge. Every part of me honed, intent on the safety of these brave forces; acutely aware of the seamless relays the conductor working through me was orchestrating.

The task was long, demanding, draining but just as the elementals never faltered neither too did my mind, my whole. I knew Donna was working with the mass of healing light which was now no longer just a chink in the blackness but a vast spreading luminous white glow opening ever further and further like a theatre curtain. And upon the stage it revealed that lives were being reunited. Souls long denied the solace of reunion and the healing balm of release into the realms beyond, were being welcomed, embraced and gently held by guiding loving lives.

The triage of welcomers would ensure that each and every one received the care and help they needed in the vast ethereal hospitals and healing places beyond. Donna would hold her focus, I knew, until the last life reached safety and the light had consumed every dark shadow and space.

As the settlement emptied and souls were released, the distress signals of trauma, heartache and pain dwindled. It felt like the land was awakening from an eternal nightmare. The deafening, sickening sounds of destruction ebbing away almost as fast as it had first taken hold. But still the elementals worked on in their relays as the core deep down still glowed, layers around the epicenter unwilling to give in, resisting with all its might.

Suddenly, in my peripheral vision, I caught sight of a hurtling spark, a speeding bright flash to the left of me. It looked and felt like a combustible fire-cracker stick of lightning. As I rapidly processed the sight like a camera on fast shutter speed, the answer came to me. "It's an errant fire spirit. It must be taken back into purpose. Now. Quickly." My heart was racing. "How, what do I do?" "Connect to a volcano – do it now!"

A part of my mind had travelled there in a nano second. Right there with the most gigantic, boiling, roaring furnace of fire power I had ever seen. It made the fire dragon energy feel like a stick of kindling. But there was no time to question, and retreat was not an option. A voice seemed to roar from within me, "Catch the fire spirit," it commanded. And to even my ethereal vision's amazement, the leaping crackling run away fire spirit was plucked by a flaming tendril and swept into the roaring volcanic belly. In my mind's eye it appeared as if a giant searing tongue had simply licked the fleeing tinder stick off the driveway and consumed it in one belching gulp.

I could still sense the voracious hunger that the very spirit of fire itself is. Hurtling towards, bush, grass and tree to feed itself, consume, rekindle and grow. The combined united will of the core of the fire had manifested within that fire spirit and like everything on planet earth hardwired to survive, it had fled towards the food that would save it from the imminent extinguishing that the relentless efforts of the air and water elementals had succeeded in sustaining.

The radiating waves of heat were now rapidly dwindling. The raging red and orange, paling, fading, shrinking. As the intense orange mass of the core surrendered to the blasts of the elements' pure will and began to fade to dying embers, the whole of my being became acutely aware of the blissful contrast in sound. The atmosphere had trembled and resonated with the raging, fierce searing echoes of roaring flames and molten heat and now the very air itself was sighing with the settled calm.

I could feel the Earth stretching, reaching to reclaim her true state. Like a film on fast forward, harmony and the land united and surged into regrowth and repair as if the most concentrated force of spring had condensed into that one space and was blissfully and eagerly seeding the new. I bathed in the aura of the land's joy and rejuvenation. The sense was familiar, comforting and deeply rewarding. I had felt this before fill the healing centre when the energy of remedy had reached into troubled souls and diffused the scars of life's traumas and pains.

But never had I been surrounded so far and wide by such intense relief pouring from the ground through the soles of my bare feet, coursing through me and heightening my senses to such acute levels. The very air itself trilled with a high whistling note that climbed and escalated in pitch, purifying the entirety of its reclaimed territory with ever brighter, finer force. And then the silence beyond hit my ears like a slap. No more screams. No more raw fear and distress. Total absence of the heart wrenching sounds of human suffering.

I glanced towards Donna, concerned as well over an hour had passed. Her stance was now relaxed but she still held the space, projecting and ensuring every soul was safely in healing hands beyond. It was tempting to ask my mind to glance into the world that was now welcoming them but the permission was not there to allow my faculties to stray. For me it was not the time to experience what lay beyond.

However it would only be a few years later when I would have my faith, trust and healing service tested beyond anything tasked with, before. Nothing would tear me apart and hold me together with a will of steel and show me the absolute beauty within the love and total care of the beyond as what lay ahead on life's path. That day those realms were sacred and special, private for the lives who would finally rejoice in its arms.

With a jolt my systems were pulled back into the epicenter of the healing focus. Visually I was now far from the house by the banks of the river. The call of water spirits quenching the very souls of themselves with the pure nectar of the home of their river. Their message was clear, 'Call to the Air elementals, bring them to the safety and cool of the river'. I remembered my duty. There were still troops on the fields and never had I witnessed such bravery and fluid working harmony as when the elements are joined in purpose.

My mind swept the entirety of the land, calling to the elementals, commanding them to the safety of the cooling balm of the river. Not until every elemental soldier had travelled to that haven and I had focused every ounce of universal healing power to those weary battered forces did the intensity that was driving my mind begin to relax. There was more to do but it was safe to rest and reflect on the miracle the very soul of the Earth had entrusted us with.

For so long the nature spirits had waited, suffering the vibrations of cruelty and harm that human hands and minds had caused. Within their permissions and capacity they held remedy in their hands but what is conceived and caused by humans must be remedied by humans too. So until the nature spirits could find just two human minds, who held correction and remedy upmost in their heart and whom they knew and could trust, all they could do was wait. And the counsel of minds waited too..... Waited for a mind that could be honed, taught, aligned, awakened until the very counsel of collective mind energy and consciousness could connect, hold and command that space through.

In beautiful ways the nature spirits had built a relationship with me and grown it until they could call me to a healing for the very essence of their own beings. And in Donna's mind and radiation they knew her intentions were clear and her sensitivity acute. Although many minds and human systems had perpetrated the harm, only one is needed to correct it. For the scale of the work, I was glad they had found two!

However, how did this all get planned? Did the mighty intelligence of minds itself plan the healing strategy? Or did the combined wisdom of Earth's air, fire, earth and water elements confer in some mysterious way how to expedite the sacred balance of their very selves? Or are they all one and within that unity we too are intended to be? With that alignment, no human hands or minds could cause war again, for the human suffering is only a part of the reality.

As I considered just how many lands and countries were crying for deep healing resolve, the space was held in a healing pause. Fine universal energies continued to surround the land, sky and water imbuing it with delighted embraces of peace. The first surges of emergent power had been like some ethereal 'medicines sans frontiers' dashing in, carrying out triage, intent on saving and resurrecting every part of Earth's battle scarred soul.

Now everything basked in a realm beyond earthly time and physical limitations and together we bathed in the rays of the sun and pure light that surpassed even its power. And inside of that dimension appeared a vaguely familiar little group of nature beings. Recollections zipped past me to the time I had first met this curious array of earth energies that my brain had struggled to give visual pictures and form to. For it then had little in its data bank of images to draw from.

I remembered it feeling akin to being cast back to a baby like state. To a time and place where the brain has to learn to cloak images with form for the very first time. Somewhere in the vast dimensions and mysteries of the brain lay its own capacity to travel to some long unused recess and pluck the strings of connections that allow the mind to feed it the vibrations of new and different frequencies. Then guide it to the process of giving them substance, outline and features.

Not for the first time I thanked my brain for its willingness to stretch, to reach, to try and allow what lives beyond physical form and sight.. And not for the first time it retorted that it 'was not mine' and continued its exploration of purchase upon the new experiences and impressions the life of brains naturally craves. Its rebuke made me smile. I was glad it was freelance! Glad that given purely permission, training and openness from whatever the 'I' is, these human systems know exactly what to do and where to take this life to find the guidance together we need.

It had made the connection to the time, to the place. Like a switch illuminating a light bulb, the reason for the appearance of the group of earth energy workers flooded through me. An old building on a farm - I had been asked to view it to see if it was suitable for a healing retreat. After spending time with the place I asked it, the land and the building itself, if that was right and intended to be. And later back, at home, as I showered and cleansed my aura, I was taken to meet the assembled little committee of beings that now visually appeared again before me.

Whilst it was not the building's destiny to become a retreat it was another rich part of the consciousness of the intuitive and instinctive responses and sensing's I had always felt for land and buildings. On the farm, that day, an internal dialogue and conversation had guided the process and I knew it felt natural and respectful to confer with whatever life and essence of the place was present and engaging, for I was a visitor in their home. When I left I promised that the lines of communication would remain open because that conversation and engagement was still present and buzzing with vibrant energy. Inside of the refreshing vigour of the shower's blessing we reconnected in their dimension, where even this brain itself was birthed into another vibration and space, and its newborn eyes widened, stretched, to see the images that lay in the strata of life we had been transported into.

There is always a head house spirit, an Earth elemental, who is in charge of the many thousands who can inhabit one place. That wise Essence life might be of the oak beam, built into the fabric of a centuries' old cottage, long ago charged with maintaining its structure and strength. Before it was felled, and chosen to be an important part of the building, the oak tree had been born from an acorn lying amidst the mossy forest floor. Born, emerged as a sapling and nourished by its forest family into adulthood and hundreds of years of the glory of the seasons it ever embraced. Through these changes, its majestic bows, every microcosm of the forest life forms became imbued within every cell of the tree.

When a space in the forest is cleared to build a cottage dwelling, neither stone, wood or soil has any choice but to surrender to its fate. Taken from the natural home and state it has always known, soil is dug and moved to become foundations. Stone meets others of its kind and is shaped and stacked to become walls and timber is sawn into doors, window frames and roof trusses. And within every single facet of the fabric of the dwelling a part of the very essence of the forest resides and thus becomes the soul life of the building itself.

When the mighty oak is felled, its weight and strength become the very core of the cottage's stability and resilience. Repurposed by human hands who value it for its ability to form and hold the very structure of what they build to shelter and protect them. However, for every stone, slat of wood and grain of earth that now together have formed a cottage, the strength they feel is in the ancient wisdom and resonance of the forest that radiates from every cell of the oak beam.

And thus, by virtue of connection and carriage of the very presence of their forest home, the elemental of the oak beams becomes the house spirit all others look to and respect as in charge.

We all know the breathtaking presence that a giant ancient tree presents from its vast spread of roots structure, to the stretching girth of its trunk and proud strong bows. Because as we stare at a magnificent beautiful physical form our impression of that presence is formed by what we physically see.

When I met the assembled committee group in their dimension and works that day, the nature being who first stepped forward to greet me was very obviously in charge. In seconds I realized, with a rush of awe, that the presence within the tree, within every life mother earth has given form to, does not emanate from its physicality, but from the very core source of its pure energy itself.

I could feel my energy body bow as I stared into the sincere, wise eyes of the head nature spirit. Every part of me sensed I already knew him. In fact, the whole gathered crowd was straining with the sheer exuberance of a puppy dog welcoming its human companion home. A part of me spoke. A life in me that had been kept alive by that invisible friend, that had once heard so naturally without filters, only to become lost to it and then jolted, shouted awake, at the first sighting of the man I was to marry. That part of me was speaking, leading the way, guiding the other parts of my awakening inner lives to meet and greet these familiar little beings.

"How do we know you?" those emerging lives asked. "Who are we? What is this life within that you already know?" Those sincere eyes, pure pools of honesty drawing me ... falling into the surrender of their space, their vibration ... So many tiny arms around my legs, my waist, holding my face as tears streamed and fell. The life within me surging with sheer exalted joy, dancing with their frequency, rejoicing, and crying. Then, finally, hearing the voice of that life rise and tear through the last of the veils that had blinded me... "Home, home, at last I am home". The flow of tears turned into a flood of relief that flowed into every corner of the place that life had been locked in and liberation ran, like children to the ice cream van, into every cell.

That most precious part of me unlocked, unleashed, unfettered, at last.

The tiny life within that stayed alive and had striven to be re-found, rekindled and had grown my life to that point. Into a myriad of incredible experiences thus far encountered. Those familiar eyes had drawn Alice to the rabbit hole and I was freefalling all the way, for nothing had ever felt so true, so right on planet Earth, ever before this moment. This is Earth. This is Truth. This is Home.

His hand was holding mine, warm with love, strong, leaving an imprint in my senses that said, "We are always here." Then the words fell from his mouth and the sparks of the connections in my aura all fused together in one lightning strike. "We know you well, We know you as Ariel."

And here they were once again. As I stood amidst that previous war torn, battle worn land that was now regenerating and recovering in shutter speed time, with the dear council of nature being friends gathered around me, those wise eyes emitted loving healing deep into my soul. "The fire spirit thanks you. Human hands had taken it away from its purpose and truth. Fire only destroys to create space and ecology for the new, for regeneration, and for rebirth. Never to serve destruction itself. It is now in the sanctuary of realignment and welcomed home."

Hearing them speak and explaining their worlds was moving and heartwarming.

"I must thank the volcano," I replied. "I am still in awe of the command that came through, and the trust, the immediacy from so far away, from a life force so vast." He again held my hand. "And now Ariel, you truly do know."

I stared deeply into the eyes of my oldest, dearest friend, with pride, the whole of me replied, "Yes, yes, now I truly do know."

It had been quite a while after that first joyous reunion that I had opened my computer and typed in 'Ariel' and what appeared filled me with amazement and delight. For Ariel is the protector of nature and Earth and elements of water, air and fire.

I rejoiced that through the miracle of trained human systems, the angel Ariel could do her work. That she had driven my passion to respect and protect Earth that had begun as an environmental campaigner and led me to dedicate myself to the healing training and the subtle and profound depth of work this spirit was sent here for. That the nature beings could feel her presence through me filled me with joy as I desperately wanted them to know we Humans care, we want to learn, we want them to know us and trust us again. But I still knew that there was more to reveal, more to discover, about my soul. And in time, as always, I would. However in that moment, yes I truly did know in every cell of my being why they knew me as Ariel. Their trust in me for that mission had sealed my destiny and my love for ever.

The group read every thought as I stood hand in hand, so glad to be with all of them again. Sweeping them all into a massive embrace, I pulled myself together and ground my bare feet firmly deep into the grass. "There is still more to do here," I announced. They all nodded vigorously. The trust in their eyes filled me with pride, for them, and deep protection.

So, silently together we all moved to the back garden of the house where Donna was standing transfixed, staring over the garden wall to the fields and skyline beyond. I took in the scene…. There was, indeed, still much more to do.

Part 2

"So why are we both still seeing the soldiers?" Donna asked. As clear as day they still lined the horizon. Severe trauma creates deeply embedded prints we both knew. And at certain times of the year the replay of those memories would surge in power and thus become visible, often out of the peripheral vision, so when you turned your head fully to look square on, the spectre would seem to disappear. However the scene was vivid on the skyline, like a long snaking scar cutting across the land, the line of troops still standing, staring, waiting. But for what?

"Follow the clues, Sue, join the dots," I muttered, pacing, searching for the connections I knew would be there. The farm land swam back into view.... Why had my mind been taken again to that farm? The insights tumbled in and only as the words spilled from my mouth did I consciously begin to realise what was being asked.

"Biodynamics," Donna swung round. "Ok," she urged. "The land has to be regenerated, protected with a new print. It's not enough, not for them, that the souls they harmed are now safe. They want to do more. It's like their honour, their duty, perhaps even their penance, to insist the land too is reborn. It will help them in the beyond, erase more of the guilt that is holding them here. The healing is not complete until it has answered their call too."

No reproach, no blame. Total absence of judgment. Only correction. True alignment and care to every detail never failed to astonish or amaze. Donna snapped her fingers. "Quartz crystal! In biodynamics quartz crystal is ground up, mixed and sprayed on the land." I surveyed the vast expanse and looked at her quizzically. "How?" She stared at me like I was losing the last of my marbles.

"Just like everything physical, quartz crystal is a specific energy vibration that has condensed into matter, in this case high force, a high energy vibration that will bring new regenerative fine force to the land... Remember the splitting of the atom lesson.." She was huffing. I nodded quickly, so as to not piss her off further. Clearly, she was channeling Einstein or something. "So, we get our minds onto that frequency and ask it to imbue the land with its energy. Unless you want to grind up crystals and walk around with spray bottles for the next month!" Thank God I rarely worked alone!

Over the next 15 minutes we chose 2 places in the garden to sit, deciding it felt right to project in two different directions. As usual with no hand book to consult, everything was done on pure instinct, and it boosted our confidence when both our faculties came up independently with similar ideas. As a work plan it wouldn't do for brain surgery, but somehow it had got us this far and out of many a dilemma together.

However, even we felt pretty out on a limb when we took up our opposing positions seated on the grass with a pile of rocks in front of us gathered from around the garden, with a chunk of crystal quartz teetering on top.

Simultaneously we turned to each other. We both sported, 'What have we got to lose?' expressions, our eyebrows couldn't travel any further towards the top of our heads. "Why do you think we felt compelled to collect these stones?" Couldn't help it, had to ask.

"Been thinking about that." Donna stretched out and picked a rock from her pile, staring at it intently. "Stones and crystals are all part of the mineral kingdom, so this pile is like a totem, an attraction, an invitation to this place, for the whole of this land's history is printed within each of these rocks. And the American Indians called them 'Stone People' and have huge reverence for them. So I don't know about you, but my mind is going to take THAT route, because I figure we need that level of respect to find a way in to attracting whatever Angelic realms quartz crystal is a part of. And like everything we start first by gathering our thoughts, so some proper value and respect is the mineral kingdom itself in all forms."

I stroked the rock closest to me thoughtfully. She was right. What history had this rock absorbed? What was its story? Whose feet had trodden it? What hands had touched it? Every moment this place had experienced was printed within it, from the turmoil of changing formation and topography, till the present day. Eons of memory, every fiber of its very being a microcosm copy of the whole experience and essence of the land itself. The feet of those very soldiers could have walked upon it, stepped over it. Reverence for the mineral kingdom to distil within me, capturing the sequins of value and wonder, ever fertile for learning and growth.

"Plus they are a part of tomorrow, here on this land. Just like house walls hold up prints, these stones will get new programming they can hold and radiate in regeneration anew. Just thoughts... might not all be well expressed but" ... Donna tailed off. "Yeah right, Yoda." I admonished. "You diss what's just come through your faculties and this rock connecting with your butt will be part of its memory. We're primed. Let's get on and focus." "Absolutely no need for violence," Donna tutted, smiling, and we turned to the task in hand.

Staring at the rocks my thoughts travelled to the American Indians worshipping the mountains, listening to the ancient whispers of the Stone People's wisdoms...

traversed the ocean to the giant statues on Easter Island... took a mental left, was it right? To the precisely engineered stones of the pyramids...hopped to India and stared at the Taj Mahal. It was true, that place just oozed wonder... and then zipped back to home soil to stare incredulously at the connection between the lives of the stone and the master mason, together guiding and being guided, joining in harmony, as the rock became refined, sculptured and moved into its new purpose as an intrinsic part of a great Cathedral.

Fascination for the very beings of stone unto themselves was buzzing in me, but I knew none of it was hitting the bullseye. "Been halfway round the bloody world," I grumbled "and it's not enough."

"Exactly," the word entered like a shotgun pellet. "Get on with the program. THESE rocks. THIS land. You are supposed to be our bloody tuning fork. VALUE this rock. Resonate with THAT crystal, ring its note and attract its Angelic source to HERE."

I could only sense the little being stamping away, muttering about, "That idiot who has got Angels flitting to all bloody parts of the globe but here." My, earth elementals were so brusque, but so right always. I shook my head embarrassed. 'A child could work that one out Sue. Get over it and get on.'

Five... Ten. The minutes passed. Fifteen and a sense of force approaching. Twenty and Donna and I simultaneously blinked our eyes open, staring together in the same direction. It was neither of the ones we had chosen to face! Pulsing showers of pale pink power cascading across the landscape, bathing the expanse in a pure, protective gentle coat. The contrast from the acrid and scarred resonance was tangible in the softness of the air on our skin and the grass beneath us. It felt that the entirety of the once traumatized land mass had entered a womb like state. A sanctuary for new growth, rebirth, within a cloister of safety. The land healing process had been brought to completion and sealed.

We arose, stretched and threw our arms around each other in a very enthusiastic tight hug.. clearly relieved but also overdosed with rose quartz crystal energy, which tends to make you very loving! "Ok," I said, as we disentangled. "Besides the fact that until the effects of this wear off, we will never actually get to concentrate on this house cleanse inside if a remotely fanciable bloke appears, I do have a serious point of focus to re-ground us. Look at the horizon and tell me - what do you see?" Donna's face relaxed further as she watched, "It's like a final surrender. What really, in their hearts, they wanted all along." As the soldiers turned and peeled away, one by one, we watched. Holding our gaze till long after they had disappeared from view. They had been locked in the purgatory of that time for far too long. A forgiving and nurturing space awaited their homecoming that would honour the best of their lives and their final act of self-chosen duty.

You always know during long days of healing work when your body relinquishes itself for a while from the almost exclusive higher system consciousness. As it drops down a gear into cruise mode the stomach immediately becomes extremely vocal. In the 'world of stomachs', their reality is that for some considerable time the call for the 'restocking of the larder' has gone totally unheard. Mine had found voice to its pangs of being ignored akin to a triplet queueing for its breast feed. Hearing the competing growls from Donna's I deduced the complaints were not unfounded! The need was to eat light though, to be able to give our best to the rest of the work ahead.

"I don't know about you, Donna," I complained, as I munched through my salad like Pac-Man on amphetamines, "but if my brain and stomach don't stop compiling a 'JUST EAT' carb laden order that would fulfil a serious case of the after dope munchies in 6 strapping blokes, I am going to have to eat this Tupperware!" Having choked on her tea laughing, her eyes resumed their focus on the grass which I knew she was considering as a dessert option. Before we both started chowing down on plastic or grazing, we grabbed our incensing kit and re-entered the house. Over 4 hours since we had stepped outside. We owed the home owner as brief a summary as we could manage on what had been healed thus far.

Courtesy thus accomplished we began to tune our dials to the house again. The hallway was now in sharp focus, the air blissfully clear of smoke. Meanwhile the front room now felt very empty. Its silence like the total sudden absence of noise that drops like a stone when a whole night's frivolities are over and the party goers all leave together. Stark contrast, but a relief for the whole fabric of the house.

It needed to be reawakened to the happiness it also held within its walls. With a certain rising sense of hope Donna trotted up the stairs, calling from the top that we might have been moved to light duties now! I had barely climbed 3 stairs before that little bubble of hope was royally burst!

A tall thin figure dressed in a theatrical long tailed black suit pushed past me down the stairs. His presence was so forceful I rocked backwards, crying out in surprise as I grabbed for the handrail. "What happened?" Donna shouted. "What did you see?" asked the lady fearfully.

"A man very tall and thin. He looked just like Fagin. Theatrically attired in a black tail suit. He travelled past me so fast and his presence was so strong it physically pushed me." "Yes, yes," she enthused. "We have him on film. The cameras have picked him up. There's more too, but he's really spooky." "Well, he's certainly not shy," I smiled, trying to lessen the drama he clearly thrived on and I had now fed into. "I guess we had better prepare to meet the rest of the cast!"

My words were having little impression. The lady still looked pensive and tense. "Are you sure you're going to be ok doing this?" "Don't worry," I reassured, "we would not be allowed to be here if we were not able to do what's needed for the remedy to do its work. We'll get on."

Finally arriving on the landing, Donna stared quizzically at the four doors leading off it. "This feels weird shit," she murmured. The atmosphere was certainly odd. Choppy and confused. Nothing seemed to fit together. It was like lots of jigsaw pieces that didn't even belong to the same picture. Eyes closed, we grounded our energy, sending long roots from the soles of our feet boring deep into the earth. Balance, breathe, and centre. The spooky dude had re-sharpened our focus. Had he sensed our auras relax? Was that stunt on the stairs just a lark for him? Or was he making us aware, providing us with a clue? Odd that Donna did not see him. A vague sense of familiarity began to tickle... I had seen someone just like him before... the pitch of the force intensified, whistling through the crown chakra. Tendrils of memory rippled evocatively, evading all efforts to haul them into the conscious mind.

Our eyes snapped open. Staring in unison at the same closed door. "Breadcrumbs," she nodded. Sometimes there would be a trail of clues to follow on the path like in Hansel and Gretel. Donna turned the handle and the door swung open. She disappeared inside.

From the threshold I realised this room held the window that had caught my attention whilst working outside. How many times had I glimpsed a boy's face at the window? The interior was arranged as a dressing room. A simple clothes rail, full length mirror, dressing table but no boy. He didn't belong here anyway. Not now, not ever that I knew. Suddenly out he stepped fully attired in old fashioned clothes... velvet breeches, short jacket. But he did not belong with that time. He turned, disappeared, only to reappear in another costume. I glanced at Donna. Her incredulous expression confirmed our visuals were synched! It was all an anachronism. None of it fitted with the time he belonged with. "Weird shit," she repeated. "Really, really, weird!"

Before another costume change happened I backed out of the room, quickly followed by Donna in fast reverse. It was an impressive maneuver from behind. She closed the door with an extra firm upward tug of the handle which made me smile. Comforting to do. But zero chance of containing anyone in the energy field who chose to have a wander!

"It doesn't fit together," declared Donna. I concurred. "It's very puzzling. What's attracting all this phenomena?" We projected visually, further and wider. Waves of energy were emitting from the house. A whole cast of mismatched characters swam into view.

"Those bloody cameras," I snapped. "The smoke and disturbance from the land emerged first. Those cameras went up after. They're adding to the problem. Drawing stuff in." Donna was on her feet. "I'm going now to get them turned off."

Left alone, I chased the threads, trying to force the tendrils of knowing into sense. To form conscious clear understanding. Other mediums and clairvoyants had mentioned how activity would increase and be magnified and amplified by cameras and sound devices. Those earth bound or in closer denser strata of energy may urge to be seen, having not yet adjusted to their new state, or seeking help to move on further. I recalled an old mill which a friend had called me to do a whole lot of settling work in after a particular TV crew of 'sensationalist' presenters had spent a day there making their program.

After 'abusing' all the poor souls there for entertainment purposes and obtaining their desired footage, they left. And everyone who then came to work the next day entered a wholly and tangibly disturbed atmosphere, which not only upset them but scared the pants off them too.

On one floor of the mill a large space, part storage and part workshop, had gone from being a pleasant room all were content to enter, to a hugely disturbed area people were fleeing from or refusing to enter. I was duly told on arrival that one room had been the main focus of the entire camera equipment as 'activity' had just kept emerging and increasing throughout the day's filming. 'Would I seek it out and make it normal again?'

It was obvious before I even climbed the stairs to that floor. The misery and distress was palpable. I almost wept at the ignorant insensitivity as I crossed its threshold. In the hunt for cheap stupid thrills and a sensationalist hour of TV 'entertainment' nigh on 20 souls had not just been disturbed but defiled. Having then got their 'pound of flesh' they had left, clutching their film rolls of increasing phenomena provoked by their very actions. How could they not stop to think these souls had lived? They had been real live people. Someone's wife, husband, son, daughter. And many had met their deaths in trauma, in accidents so rife in the mills. The man hanging from the beams could have been murdered or he could have taken his own life. Do we stand and gawp in morbid curiosity, or do we hold a space for that which will end his suffering?

A heady soup of disturbed prints and memories in the walls, and souls locked in past time, had all been drawn out and into that one space, creating an epicentre of presence. I went from angry at being charged with the duty of 'ethereal scrubber' and cleaner upper purely due to other human beings' irresponsibility to deciding it was a perfect opportunity for healing resolve for those lives and the building, and to just crack on. That work had certainly proved how unhelpful cameras are where activity is rife.

The sound of Donna's return broke through my reflections. "Cameras are off," she declared, sinking to the ground and stretching her legs out somewhat wearily. Plonking myself down facing her I relayed the links and pathways we'd been led to so far. As always her innate intuition was working overtime. As was her ability to pull on the threads in exactly the way needed. Some people are weavers. They spin the finest of clues and hints together to form a seamless thread. Then together you work those threads until a tapestry is formed that tells the story just how it is. Her inner compass of the weaving faculties was pivoting and the needle was soon pointing at a loose thread I had been led away from.

"We both saw the boy, all the 'extras'. We both knew it didn't fit and you've explained that. But all day, even before I got here, we have been in synch, totally in harmony. The 'gap' is the Fagin character and why did he look dressed up? And why was that boy changing his appearance? You saw him and I didn't. Or couldn't. So what is he telling you about this eclectic mix of phenomena that's causing disturbance here?" She was right. Pretty much always bang on the nail.

Back to searching the mind, petitioning for guidance. "Something keeps giving me the word 'shapeshifter' " I said finally. "And somewhere before I have seen an apparition just like him." I was fighting tiredness, but Donna seemed to be on her third wind of the day! It was in her sails and she was not about to travel any new oceans alone. "What does shapeshifter mean? And where did you learn that before?" The thread travelled further, firing more neurons. Then met a serious knot. I looked glumly at Donna. "They are advanced or magician type souls that can change form, completely alter their appearance and present themselves in different guises. That's what the 'boy' was all about, who I'm damn sure is not a boy. However he was giving us a clue, so must be working on the light side of the energy field. Because some are seasoned in working for the 'other side' of the energy realms.

"They could have practiced dark arts, been amidst the magic circle, secret societies and used energy in negative or less constructive ways. So, with any of that ilk in the mix I am pretty darn sure they can outwit any cleansing we try to do and probably fry our asses in the process.

Potentially we are screwed."

Defeat was never an option. But taking high healing friends into unsafe territory was not either. The coarse energy destroys the fine. Donna broke through my gloom, "You have not answered all of the question." She stretched her legs and stared at me persistently. I stared back at her, like she was a Royal pain in the ass! Good friends in life often are. "Which bit?" I snapped.

She leaned forward, "Gather your mind. After you saw 'Fagin' you said to the lady very clearly that we would not be here if we could not enable what will bring in the cure - your words? Or his? Or what he represents? So where did you hear that term 'shapeshifters' explained?"

The needle travelled through the knot and the thread began to fizz. Like a firework it exploded into colour and flames. And there I was, back in a pretty village, sitting in a hall amidst a huge circle of healers. "The Ascended Masters' Course with Janet," I blurted out.

Donna sat back. "Tell me what happened."

"It was at the very beginning of the day. We were all sitting in a circle, it was a big gathering. Janet and two other healers, a man and a lady, were orchestrating the workshop. The first process we did was a cleansing meditation and were asked to visualize a fire in the middle of the circle and draw it to us to cleanse our energy and prepare. Everyone went deep into the meditation and it got really strong very quickly. I connected to the fire and a trail blazed across to me to purify and cleanse, but then I became aware that I could see everyone's trail of fire from the core dividing the circle into these beautiful segments and it was mesmerizing.

"But then the fire spread into an entire ring forming a whole outer circle around the backs of the chairs, so we were all encompassed in this circle of fire too. It was incredible to see. And then all of a sudden this magician in a top hat, waistcoat and tailcoat, sprang out of the fire. He leaped right in front of me, spread his arms out theatrically and shouted 'Ta Da' and then shrank in front of my eyes and disappeared.

Even my third eye was blinking at that one! But then he reappeared, danced around the whole circle until he was in front of me again, did this deep theatrical magician bow and then just jumped back into the flames. God, I have seen so many things and been told 'Always say what you see' but that was stunning. So clear, intense, comical and happened so fast too." "So what happened then?" "Well, we emerged from the process and lots of people fed back their experiences with the meditation, but no one mentioned seeing the fire spread or the magician, not one other person.

"And they were going to move on but something insisted I say what I'd seen. So, I just said, 'Something really awesome happened but I don't understand what I've just seen', and I began to recount what had occurred.

"The more I told the more excited and animated the gentleman sitting with Janet got. Finally, for him, I finished because he was bursting by then! He said, 'You have just seen Merlin.' This guy had really studied Merlin a lot.

"Well, we were at a Course connecting with Ascended Masters after all and Merlin is a hugely Ascended Master! So he told us that Merlin is a Master of appearance and disappearance. And that he is also a shape shifter so can appear in any form he chooses, a magician being of course a most favoured one in many guises. I was stunned into silence by then, and he was saying to me, 'Merlin has without doubt just appeared to you, have you worked with Merlin before?'

"I can see it all still now as clear as day and I had to say I really didn't know if I had worked with Merlin before, not consciously anyway." Donna was smiling a lot. "Until today." The pennies started to drop. "My head had become a piggy bank." "Oh my God, the fire, the orchestration of the elemental forces! Merlin has been working with us and through us all day. Now I understand the clarity, the ability, and the capacity. The response from the Volcano."

The sheer power of Merlin and earth together and we had been their human agency. She brought me back to earth and to the task in hand, "Fabulous. You have answered the question of what to do. Merlin the master of all masters of shape shifting is waiting to be consciously included to complete this cleanse and end this. He can with us, just as we only can with him.

Or the realm Merlin represents. So shall we light this meditation fire and let him do what he is waiting to do?"

So, there on the landing of the house, where just hours before all had worked to put out a fire that had burned for centuries, we lit another with our minds and watched as a dome of protection covered the house. And Merlin worked his magic, dispersing energies that did not belong, ushering souls into the arms of those waiting and banishing the shape shifters safely. With the ease and proficiency of clear exacting guidance, an effect only a highly evolved ascended master could bring. We held our concentration for as long as those proficient and capable realms needed us to, our relief palpable between us to indeed have 'friends in high places'. The house seemed to sigh and stretch deep down into its foundations. It was as if each brick had been uneasily repelled for so long by the traumas it lay amidst and now calm bathed it from its very roots to the eaves at last.

By the time we had finished shielding, incensing and completing the cleanse almost 8 hours had passed. Standing in the front room again it was hard to believe that it was only that morning when we had begun, for the sheer scale of the work accomplished was immense.

My thoughts shifted to the Mother and her children and the beautiful sense of peace and joy they were now united in. Never had I thought when I said those words, "I want to be a healer," that the journey would hold such huge, testing and profound gifts of learning. I did not think of what might lie ahead. It was overwhelming to just wonder at the pathway to this moment now.

Donna appeared in the doorway rattling my car keys. "Come on you. We need to get home before we crash." She was right. Again. For as soon as we drove away the focus of our systems would begin to distil back into more 'usual' everyday spaces and all that had been held at bay would drop in with a bang!

The payoff of being held in continuous function in our higher systems so intensely for so long was already starting to bite. And this would be a crash, like two addicts without a stash! Already my head was throbbing, thick and dense with the mother of all coarse force headaches cleansing and healing work rewards you with. Through comes the high force and you then by default 'cop' the low... the trade-off of new lamps, all bright, for old lamps! The joy of being a human hoover!

My brain was wincing at the banging fog surrounding it. We needed long hot showers to clear our entire energy field and cleanse our chakras fully. Our bodies were dead beat and our auras were sludge! The last cleanse of the day had to be us and we had to do it well to stay well. To continue to work to this level our self-care had to equal every elevation, to stay fit to serve.

Plucking the keys from her hand, I cast one more look around, sending gratitude to the land, the Elementals, the High Essences, to Merlin. The lady thanked us profusely and as she closed the door I got hold of Donna's arm. She turned, anticipating a hug. "Have you told her to keep those sodding cameras off?" I asked. She roared with laughter.

"I see the rose quartz has worn off then! Yes, I have and let's hope she heeds it. However, whatever, our work here is DONE!" Glad of her earthy common sense, I threw my arms around her. "We have got to stop doing this insane work together. I daren't even imagine what will happen next."

"Well, you won't have much time to wonder. Another job came in!" I drew away. My face said 'NO' but my systems leapt. Training and more training. They just loved to do this work. "Diary out tomorrow. First let's clean up and get a long sleep…and oh my God, food! I am ravenous now."

As we drove away I wondered at the mysteries of how Donna had been brought to me as a client in that first healing room. All the experiences we had travelled through to bring us to creating a Healing Centre together. Which was where? Where on our journey were we?

"I still don't really know how you would describe what I am growing up to be," I declared out loud. "But shit, if I had told that teacher I wanted to be the Protector of the Fairy Realms and work for Merlin the Magician, by God she'd have had me one finger typing a hundred times, 'I will consider my career options sensibly'."

Laughing with the Nature Elementals all the way home, I followed the life plan I had always trusted…let the next day arrive and take me to what it chose to teach me. And little Earth time passed before I discovered that Merlin may be a Master of the Elements, but that was the tip of the iceberg of what lay ahead.

Chapter 9

Growth

From the very first healing sessions Donna came for, something extra and curious began. Her natural attunement arose, our systems harmonized and another part of the organically unfolding plan began.

So, by our fourth meeting the Essences were introducing us to tasks that they needed us to work together on. Before long our regular sessions purely revolved around healing redress for wherever they called our minds and faculties to, that week. They had set us on a path of working closely together for the next few years. Those early days still happily ensconced in the charity therapy room, held some fascinating experiences and began to immerse us in the value of the power of two calibrated systems working on the healing's behalf.

During the first two years of working together, Donna and I set up the healing practice as a community interest company with the purpose of providing as many low-cost treatments as possible.

In the evidence of the natural flow of life, it was a certainty that if a person was meant to be led to our door for assistance, then there would no doubt be a good reason. However, money, or lack of it, could be a troublesome 'blockage' to the universe's divine plans and channels. And so often, in the greatest times of need, ill health causes funds to be in even shorter supply.

With the will to proffer the best bridge we could for remedial realms to reach as many as possible, the CIC had been formed. And with the great practical help again of family and friends, we created a small healing centre.

But, a short 18 months later we were on the move again! The new premises were extremely spacious, with high ceilings and large windows. Exactly the dimensions and light that serves energies so well. Another long labour of love ensued, stripping walls and redecorating and refurbishing the old wooden floors. Yet again the building thrived on the thorough attention until eventually we had three large therapy rooms and a spacious workshop area too.

It seemed that the powers in charge had neatly orchestrated not only doubling their staff but also much more space to grow. What a generous warm soul that building had. As each pristine room emerged to completion, so too did the nature elemental presences blossom. Before long they were making us very aware of their delightful effervescence and feeding our systems with their directives and wishes. In reality we knew that practically we did not need such a huge therapy centre. But the essence realms and nature spirit worlds did!

Each day the place filled up more and more with energetic well-being and new arriving force. Yet again they had led the way knowing full well how to serve their needs to provide a first-class service for all who came. As their healing sanctuary evolved, they overflowed with the desire to express their abundance and appreciation too! The very first gesture we had made, upon collecting the keys, was to set up a simple devotional space in the corner of one of the rooms. Upon arriving to do so, a white feather already lay right in the intended spot.

Of course, one of the many ways they have of communicating their presence and of telling us our thoughts are heard. The more redecorating work and healing sessions we did, the more and more the feathers manifested until one evening I began to clean my room and realized that the floor next to the wash stand under the window was a total blanket of feathers.

Glaring at the many pigeons outside, the thought was launched before I could quell it, 'Some of these must be blowing in. They can't all be gifts.' The words had barely vibrated around my aura before the retort shot in. "Oh really, that's what you think do you?!"

I reprimanded myself aloud. I apologized profusely. But I knew it would make absolutely no difference now. I had shown them a fault line, a flaw in my belief, and it was their duty and delight to sort that and me out! Thus the game ensued.

The door to Donna's therapy room was directly opposite mine and lay open. Despite the semi- darkness I saw the paper shade on the large floor lamp by the door begin to visibly move. As I entered I felt the little beings dart away, their mischievous laughter rippling in the air. Smiling, I reached down and turned on the lamp. The bulbs popped with a mighty bang. Turning around I threw the switch on the landing lights and another bulb popped.

The power surges when energies climb, always blows bulbs, even trips fuses and we had learned to stock a huge supply of bulbs because it happened a lot. Now united in their game of proving their presence they clearly intended to show me how forceful and abundant it was. "Ok guys," I said aloud as I climbed down off the step ladder onto the landing, "I hear you, I've got the message," and flicked the switch again.

Another bulb blew. Another ripple of giggles. "If you're going to blow bloody all of them do the remaining one now," I complained, ascending the steps with another replacement. A pensive pause. It wasn't over, but like scolded children they sensed the limits and would work out how to direct their mischief another way. Third bulb duly replaced, they lent their effervescent willingness to tidying up whilst I made it very clear how much I believed in them all and valued them greatly.

Believing that would be the end of that lesson, what met me as I walked into the therapy centre's kitchen the next morning was a feat of resourcefulness. Total proof of their wonderful humour that sealed any cracks in my belief instantly and irrevocably.

On the kitchen worktop a row of unfixed granite tiles sat and there, propped but upright and proud between them, was a very tall pure white feather. Astonishment turned to peals of laughter and tears of happiness. What wonderful humour and ingenuity and what a special way to ensure the lesson had been learned!

Later, having related to Donna a full account of their antics, we left the centre for a couple of hours to get ready for that evening's workshop. On return, Donna headed into the kitchen ahead of me, stopped abruptly and called, "So was your feather like this?"

I shot into the kitchen to be met by an identical scene. Another feather propped totally upright, between the granite tiles. It declared with cheeky style and wit, 'We enjoyed your explanation, but we'll show Donna anyway, so she's really got the message too. And of course, a gift'. It was clear that the building's nature elementals were enjoying themselves immensely. Loving being known and recognised. Appreciating their new lives and purpose.

"Well, it's very clear who is in charge," I said, "and as literally walls do have ears, we may as well wave these white feathers and surrender. They totally have the upper hand and I, for one, am very happy about that." With a little footnote about the weekly lightbulb bill Donna agreed.

Once our mindful awareness of the elementals present from both, the building and land, had firmly taken root, our heightened sensitivity began to recognise that we were always searching through our extensive choice of music for the same few CD's.

It took little to work out that the building loved to hear ladies' voices raised in song. Something in its history had been awoken and yearned for those pure tones to fill its whole being again. It evoked the memory of a fabulous book, read some years before about a couple who realized their dream and bought a castle in Wales. It was in a very poor state of repair, having been dreadfully and insensitively treated by being turned into a nightclub in its latter years. That failed miserably, so it then lay empty and abandoned in a sad and undignified state.

They rescued it by pouring years of passion and commitment into it. The combination of struggle, hard work and their pure intention not only brought its physical stature back to life but re-awoke its soul and spirit too.

It was a captivating account of the alchemists human beings can be when they care to listen and attune themselves to what the land and building itself calls for, rather than enforce their own ideals and preconceived designs upon it. That castle captured them, because elementals, the very soul and spirited life of the place itself knew, with and through that couple, they would dance together and flourish again.

During the early times of living in the castle in its still semi-derelict state, the gentleman had swept and cleaned every day and filled every room with music. It was not background entertainment but done with a clean pristine intention to find the music from the eras the castle sought to reconnect to. To energetically awaken the links to pathways of memories and join it with the times of its greatest wellbeing. To re-evoke the presence of its grandeur and pride in self.

Yes, restoration truly was a wooing and courting of the very essence of its splendour. A constant love affair, which, with each emerging signal, resonating a same-same note, strengthening every value that every life had radiated with. The art of evocation to the abundance of lives who had been glad of its shelter and employment. Music became the medium within the ceremony of rekindling and rebirthing of the castle's very presence.

When I stayed there some years later with my Mother, we both indeed found that the most joyful trace of its history was very intact. In one bedroom I dreamed the whole night of children playing and laughing, totally moved into the many happy years it had spent as the nursery playroom.

Every toy and rocking horse was as clear as day and whilst not a restful night, it was a vividly clear experience of being taken along the timelines and allowed a glimpse of the castle's own life and soul.

My Mum awoke bleary eyed announcing she would have slept well if children had not been bouncing on the bed all night! We had the fortune of spending our last night in another bedroom, Mum was soon fast asleep.

As I lay reading, a form passed by the bed and as it jumped up I knew a little ghost cat had sought us out for company. It duly turned around a few times before settling onto my stomach and curling up contentedly. I thus dared not to move as it was such a delightful experience and went to sleep with the tangible warmth of its energy and gentle purring settlement.

Upon waking I found Mum half hanging out of bed scanning the floor. "I just saw a cat jump off the bed and go past me," she said. "But there is not a cat here." Always lovely to be able to confirm that the eyes are not deceiving and indeed a cat had been with us all night. The whole historic record of that castle was certainly not only restored but in harmony and peace too.

So, as our building bathed its own soul in the sounds of ladies' voices raised in song, we added more of its choice to the music collection and I began to ask if we could share in that pleasing memory with it. Soon a lady moved into my sphere of vision. She loved to sit by the window in the room that was now my therapy space.

Her print was strong, she had loved the building as much as it adored her. As she watched the busy activity of the market place below, her voice raised in song resonated around the walls, amplified by the acoustics of the high ceilings. The echoes of her memory had been strengthened by the music. It had stirred the harmony and settlement in the soul of the building that singing is so well known to cause.

Around the same time we began to sense a regular presence on the stairs and landing. Frequently we would open our therapy room doors to welcome a visitor only to find that no one had entered. The presence was much stronger when we worked late into the evening and we felt sure it was a man who was watchful of our safety. He was there by choice and belonged, so we embraced him as part of the energy family and pressed on.

Before long the day arrived when the entrance door opened and closed but some minutes passed before there were footsteps climbing the stairs. I had not met this client before and her first words were, "Do you know there is a man who greets you at the door? He told me he is guarding this place, and you, and everyone who enters is checked. There will be no one who will get past his energy who is not meant to be here."

It was the confirmation we always appreciate receiving. As a long-established stage medium, the lady had been unfazed and found it very gracious to be welcomed at the door. She then asked if I knew about the lady who sat by the window, and loved to sing. It felt good to be able to acknowledge them both with another life who understood and respected these realms, but also had no prior connection to the building.

"They both feel really powered at this time and belong here, want to be here," I explained to her. "I would know, wouldn't I, if they needed help to move on?" The medium's eyes were intense, knowing. "They chose to be close in this vibration. Their presence here is strong at this time because it is intended that they work in service to the atmosphere and safety of this place. It's special, unique. When, if, that is no longer fitting or needed they will no longer manifest here.

You will know when you meet those who are earthbound and have never passed over. And when you do, you will help them move on."

A week later the medium's words rang in my ears. As we answered a call to a house that was stuck in the past. And faced the challenge of the life holding it there who was in no hurry to move on! Our next lessons about helping earthbound souls were about to commence!

Chapter 10

Rebirthing

Part 1

On entering, the house appeared to be an accommodating home for five lively occupants. 3 frenetic young children and 2 busy parents. After the obligatory welcoming cup of tea, we set out our incense, chimes and clearing sprays and took a moment to sense where it felt right to begin and agreed that upstairs was calling the loudest.

Donna was still amidst a conversation with the home owners, so I set off upstairs. About two thirds of the way up I was brought to an abrupt stop. The searing sharp pain shooting through my right hip was agony. Groans were stifled as my focus was pulled to the landing above where an elderly lady stood. She was clad in an old pink dressing gown and a hairnet. "Ok, six occupants," I muttered. "And boy, have you got one dicky hip, too, love!"

Clearly the time had come to help her onwards. The healing energies were making the message all too painfully clear! Reaching the top of the stairs I heard Donna starting to climb them and being a good friend decided to observe if the same thing happened to her! Lo and behold, on the very same stair she buckled and cried out in pain. "Right hip?" I asked. "God, yes, that kills," she gasped. "Same thing happened to me," I said cheerily. She threw me an unimpressed scowl. "Well you could have warned me." Her voice trailed off as she too saw the lady.

"Oh great," she sighed. "Pink dressing gown and hairnet. And one very bad hip. They have just told me that they have often seen an old lady in their bedroom and the landing," she continued, regaining her balance and hobbling up the remaining stairs.

We didn't need to confer to know we both had sensed the same thing. She was very strongly attached to the house, her home, and you could feel it straining, needing to move forwards and out of the time frame she locked so much of its energy into.

She was strong, and stubborn. It would be no easy task to help her onwards. We readied ourselves, petitioned unseen friends and the house spirits to please help when we summoned them and entered the bedroom to begin. The presence of its past hung in the air defying all physical updates. So, the layout seemed at odds with the blueprint it held. Having never found ourselves in a situation quite like this before, where we had to instigate the process of trying to encourage a life to move on, who very clearly would resist it I followed the cues of my training. Having first energetically shielded the walls, floor and ceiling to create a protected space to work, we let the guidance emerge. "We'll basilica first." Donna nodded and padded downstairs to light the charcoal and add the basilica 'granules' which would powerfully disinfect the atmosphere. Meanwhile, I fired silver force into each corner of the room where heavy static gathers, then loudly clapped each one out to disturb and break up the coarser force they were holding.

After mentally projecting blue smoke filling the room floor to ceiling and visually dissipating that through the open windows, I sensed the room again. The air felt less sticky and cloying. As the blue smoke had gathered up the debris, I had audibly registered lumps and clumps being dispersed out into the fresh air beyond. It sounded like balls of fluff passing through a hoover pipe. Thanking the plants and trees around for their assistance, as some of that force would be taken in as food for them, and sending any that needed transmuting to a trusty cosmic recycling bin, I projected to the House spirits that my noisy work was over!

Clapping really helps to break the dense build up that accumulates from the electromagnetic waste electrical wiring and equipment, phones and computers emit. In addition to that there is the residual exhaust our bodies release during the purification ceremony that sleep is. Throw in too the emissions from emotional huffs and puffs... anger, argument, frustration...human fumes we are all subject to in lesser or greater degrees. Stir in some stress and frantic rushing to get ready for work on time. Then blend in driving the vacuum cleaner through at Formula One speed whilst shouting to the kids to stop killing each other. Sprinkle a healthy dose of confused rapid thinking about what to do for tea and fit in parents' evening into the mix and then top it with a popular gripe of why is there never any visible floor in any kid's bedroom and the result is a really heady soup of coarse static waste that favours hiding in the dark corners of the room and hovers low around the floor.

Denser energy sinks, so clapping and stamping breaks it up. Exactly why a child will stamp their feet whilst having a tantrum in an effort to disperse the outplay of their emotional outburst. So, it served a purpose to be noisy, but as the elementals and finer energy realms are repelled by it, warning them before commencing is always wise, and considerate. They will retreat and return once the task is done.

By the time Donna had completed circling the room anti clockwise, with the basilica smoke puttering around the walls, the room had opened up energetically into a clear bright working area. The anti-clockwise motion draws down and out. Hopefully, later we would be able to set and seal a new start and atmosphere with other incense in a clockwise direction. But first we had one challenging energy form to tackle and I for one was not relishing the task. The hair net, pink dressing gown and dicky hip were just old lady disguises! She had been a force to be reckoned with in life and it felt like dying had only condensed it further into one strong wall of force!

Donna's face also spouted a prize-winning look of consternation. "This is how people look," I told her, "When the Doc says, 'This broken arm needs re-setting before it is plastered, so this will hurt a bit'!" Donna closed her eyes. "You are a veritable font of delight today! All birthday cake and jelly in your world! Come on, take a deep breath and let's get on."

Sometimes you can hear the nature spirits speaking through each other and calling us to attention. I breathed deeply, "Ok, I am going in!" "Let's party," Donna muttered and silence enveloped as we focused together.

Up to that moment I have never considered, from our earth-bound souls' perspective, what it must look like when two other souls raise their energy bodies to meet and vibrate on the same level. Judging from the lady's face and stance it appeared as if she thought she had gained two lodgers and was adding up what to charge us in rent! In that moment two insights consumed my whole focus. Firstly, this was her home and we were visitors. Next time mindful introductions should be transmitted first. Secondly we were amidst meeting the entirety of the energy of a life lived so we either proceed with due care and respect to that or the way will be barred. High force has equally high standards. Align your mind and heart to meet that and you will be allowed to enter and play your part. Approach casually and this life, and what is attending, misses this window of timing that's been carefully orchestrated that day. Those respectful hesitations proved to be invaluable.

As the internal switches of alignments tweaked into place, the energy softened and elevated. The clear channel of the clean issues of Developed Agencies working from on High filled the rooms, enriching and joining with the myriad of endemic nature spirits, a unique combination to that home and that land. Energetically reaching out to the lady I transmitted, "We are here to help you. You missed your window of time to pass over from here. Is there something you would like to do? Or say to us?"

She walked slowly from the landing into the bedroom. I wondered what other energies she could see in the room. Symbiotically, as she entered, the bedroom shifted into the time and space she was locked in. The layout was so different. Now, instead of a chest of drawers, I faced a heavy dark wood wardrobe and my feet stood on an old worn patterned rug that partly covered a Lino floor. The bed stood high, bedecked with hand knitted coverings, with the sturdy unrelenting shape of a long bolster forming a solid elevated mass, part obscuring a wrought iron bedstead. There she stood, lovingly, longingly surveying her bedroom. This was not stubbornness. Yes, she exuded willfulness and strength, all aspects of a character built from living through war torn times. This lady had been a daughter, a wife, a mother and this was her home.

Her source of sanctuary and safety. The storehouse of memories mirrored those held in her mind. I had to emit every desire and permission for her to do this her way.

Holding my focus, I whispered to Donna, "She has allowed me into her space. What do you see?" Quietly Donna explained, "She was reading a letter. It broke her heart. The news that her husband had been killed in action. This house was everything she had of him, of his memory. She clung to it until she was attached too strongly to go. Her husband is here waiting to take her over." I could see a portal open, waiting. And there he stood, in his uniform, just as she had seen him last. "Just ask him to wait. Hold that door open. There is something she needs to do."

The lady had opened the wardrobe and was carefully choosing some clothes. Somehow the process felt it had once been very special but it had been a long time since the old pink dressing gown had been shed. Her energy lifted with each item donned. She combed out her hair and placed her hat expertly on her head. "Well?" she demanded, standing determined before me, "How do I look?"

Resplendently clad in her Sunday best, she had an aura of mild irritability mixed with self-conscious concern. Of course she wanted to look her best to leave the house. No one popped to the shop in their pajamas or joggers in those days!

My eyes travelled from her shiny black small, heeled shoes, to her tan stockinged legs, up to her A line back shirt and matching jacket with a crisp white blouse underneath. It was buttoned to the neck and embellished with a small black ribbon bow. Neat curls peeped from beneath her black small brimmed hat, modestly decorated with another small ribbon trim. I fixed her in my gaze and smiled broadly, "You look amazing. Perfect. Are you ready to go?"

Sadness clouded her face again. The hold was so great. "Help us house spirits," I implored. "Release her all you can. I know you love her dearly. Help her to let go." "He's holding out his hands," Donna said quietly. "You have to urge her to see him now. It feels like there isn't the energy in me to wait much longer."

Propelling her focus towards that portal took every ounce of strength I had. Many hands were literally pushing, guiding, urging her towards that doorway and the closer she got the stronger its vacuum of power became. Then everything happened in an instant. She saw her husband, cried out, and reached for his hands. Joy and relief flooded from him as he grasped her tightly. And then they were gone. The silence was deafening as the turbo powered force that had been emitting from the portal died away. We watched dumb struck as the portal shrank, our systems still projecting healing and thanks. Just as that sacred shimmering bridge between two worlds closed up, her face swam back into view. Lines of age and sorrow, now laughter wrinkles. Eyes twinkling with delight and mischief, she said, "It's marvelous over here. If I had known I would have gone sooner." And then she was gone, the portal sealed shut and I sank gratefully onto an Ottoman behind me. I felt like a well wrung out sponge! Every ounce of my energy was sapped and I could feel every system shouting with shock from the draining it had caused on all the accumulators.

Donna handed me a glass of water. She had 'arrived' back into the room a few minutes before me, but was using a wall to prop herself up and hastily glugging down water. The sheer intensity of the process had left us parched.

We stayed in the silence knowing on many levels we were being checked, recalibrated, replenished, so being receptive, still and quiet was all they needed for a while. The 'hold' would break, the energy would change again, when their gracious care and attention was complete. It took a while but then pitches ebbed, vibrations calmed and quietened.

'Bless you all and thank you' emitted from all within me. "It gets easier," the guidance assured. "Your systems know how much energy this takes, so will know next time how to prepare." That makes sense, I mused. As whenever you intend to do a job you have done before, your faculties know how much energy it takes to do it and if they are healthy and able to, they will summon and manufacture that in advance, ready to enable you to carry out the task. My thoughts traced along the thread, remembering all the years of different training in honouring the human design's exacting service and dedication. Working away at that one simple, yet huge truth within the importance of following through practically with what you intend.

Otherwise, forever, all within listens, responds, prepares and provides, faithfully honouring its side of the deal. However, if you, the life it serves, keep changing your mind or allow the habits of not following through on promises and intentions to become your default pattern of choice, then the inner systems cease to trust. They turn away, feeling let down, unable to know when to trust intentions, promises. And then the energy is not there to summon. The willingness and capacity to do so has been turned off. In a million moments every day that working relationship can either be enhanced and grown, or withered away.

Helping lives onwards, who have held strongly to the familiarity of their home, and the magnetic hold of physical earthly possessions and memories, was a whole new pitch Donna and I were playing on. So, we would have to run up and down it a few times still for everything within to get the measure of it. For the body to produce enough puff and stamina to carry us to the final whistle with energy left over to do victory star jumps too!

However, we had succeeded. A good service for many lives and the home had been achieved. I was just allowing a few imagined star jumps as Donna broke the silence. "Boy did that take it out of us! And wow, have we just had some healing given us." I nodded. My face still held a quite stupefied expression. "How the heck did you manage to persuade her over? What was it she wanted to do?" We sat together to learn and understand as much as we could. Eventually we both stood and stretched, unanimously agreeing with all present, it was time to complete the house cleanse.

Working in harmony we followed the same pattern, shielding, clapping, purifying with silver force and blue 'smoke'. At last it was time to invite the new into the clean spaces now created. To allow the house that 'final for now up-date' and become present. Donna's hand hovered over the four containers of incense granules, waiting to be moved to the one the house spirits would choose. Sanctuary- blue frequency- to create a cool, reflective, calm and safe atmosphere.

Priory-White frequency-neutral, steadying, contemplative, deepening, almost secular. Or would it be Abbey-yellow frequency-ambience, joining, merging, connecting. Much denser in vibration but excellent for dwelling and forging connections between groups and families. Or Cathedral- green and enlivening, awakening, powering speed actively and mentally. Perfect for spontaneity, to lift and bring in zest and life.

"Sanctuary and Priory mixed," Donna declared. The familiar aromas rose with the puttering smoke as granules melted on hot charcoal, as Donna worked clockwise through every room, and I climbed the stairs. No pain, landing pristine clear and empty. My mind joined the energy of the house and for a moment it stayed connected to the blueprint of its 'former' days.

And then the pictures flashed through, faster and faster, travelling through the many lives and moments that had happened since within its walls. The prints in its soul and foundations provided a fast forward display, like a projector running at speed through slide shots. Then, through the front door, the present family arrived. Spilling excitedly into the home, packing boxes all over, the house in disarray. Children's completed bedrooms appeared, the living room took shape and before even two minutes had passed, I could see the family ensconced at the dining table, eating and laughing together.

The hold was broken. The house energies were all together. In harmony, calibrated, present and up to date. Another house was settled, the disparities and oddities that had haunted and affected the wellbeing of the whole were gone. Donna beckoned me downstairs, "Our work here is complete."

"In this house," I smiled, "but I sense the next ones are already lining up." "Phones already ringing and next diary dates are in," she laughed. "That's one energy realm we work with that certainly doesn't hang around."

Thus, just a few days later our kit was packed and we were off again.

Part 2

Just as every living being has a different character and personality, so do buildings. Their design, time of 'birth', the materials used and the land they are sited upon all either enhance, harmonize and cause a glow of well-being and belonging, or conflict with each other, and radiate disparity.

In the latter case, the building's occupants will never feel well. 'Sick building syndrome' affects many buildings and it is well known that in those whose workplace is so afflicted they will suffer more sick days, never mind how it affects productivity, focus and ability too.

Design and construction, without any consideration or knowledge of what ecology and energy is, as Culpeper would say 'Like a Miner working without a lamp'. Within the land lie layers and layers of history. Echoes and prints which may, or may not, enhance and serve the present occupants well. The rock structures may be soft, like sandstone, or hard like granite. Each will resonate, and create different atmospherics. Varieties of minerals and metals, each with unique elemental lives, create vast ranges of frequencies which will either serve the purpose of that place and resonate in harmony, or will resist and cause a myriad of issues.

And, all this before people add their auras, their energy and processes to the mix! Using reclaimed materials will carry in, additionally, the energy prints and history of the place and people it has originated from. Low lying ground and valleys hold and contain energies, which, with the right purpose in mind can be very positive, but not if anything toxic or polluting is sited or living there! Amidst distorted, disruptive lives, or lines of pylons, a poisonous soup, a veritable cooking pot of trouble, will soon bubble and spill over.

Living above an underground stream may purify and refresh, but not if the source of it passes under the local prison or hospital before it reaches you. Or the colour works above are discharging waste and fouling its very being! We are physical and energetic beings and therefore our ecology MATTERS A LOT! To our mental and emotional health and growth. To our physical well-being. To our human potential.

Yet right from being a child we are often crammed into nursery spaces, day centres and schools that have neither been built with the thought of the tender young occupants, or whose walls still ring with the sounds of canes still punishing children.

Banks of computers stand, anachronisms amidst the embedded prints of chalks and slates and the echoes of voices raised, learning by rote. Every form, every physical structure produced has an energetic life and being too. You can happen across an enchanting old cottage nestled in the woods and feel how its presence is accepted and its character belongs. How all this surrounding life and the land resonates in synchronicity, in happy unified communion. For it has been built of the very fabric of the surrounding nature and land. It is of that place, endemic and true.

Then gaze upwards, high, high above, to the ancient castle, its silhouette engraved into the skyline. The huge rocky strata it stands solidly on is indistinguishable from the fortress walls. Where does the hilltop end and castle begin? As part of the rock, they are one. Inseparable. Radiating impenetrability together.

But what about the contrast? Of sharp angular concrete block building housing hovering uncomfortably above land that can neither recognise nor accept it? Held in the iron grip of metal girders, with dark grey tinted glass, creating windows that defy their very purpose and repel all natural light. What nature spirit has this construction birthed? What beings could this possibly have created? Sick ones? Ugly, depressed, unhappy ones? Because the very essence and soul life of the building is ill. And disease will be prevalent in all who inhabit it.

Just as farmers are the gardeners of the landscapes, designers, builders, joiners, and architects are midwives of energy and doctors to our human design. When purpose governs design, and empathy and passion guide, what is created is a symphony. The eyes rest upon it and smile. Every sense runs towards it and bathes in its whole. But most of all, Earth embraces it and her soul life blends with it so all become one.

As we pulled up outside the next house we were glad to see it sitting happily on its street, well established and outwardly content. The interior was equally cheerful, with an eclectic mix of reclaimed furnishings, radiating in harmony from the investment of care and skill to their rescue. Within it a happy family unit thrived, so all appeared to be in well-being together. However, they had a sense of some residual energy that was calling for attention, so being in tune and empathy with their surroundings they had decided to see if their instincts ran true.

Now the rhythms of our vibrations inside of regularity and patterns practised over time become ceremonic. Indeed, it turns into our own 'Order of Service' in how we proffer ourselves in the purpose to serve all that petitions for remedy, and all that awaits to respond. And that remedial realm has a deep love to the devotion of Ceremony. There it waited, in the wings, as the incense and cleansing kit were neatly laid out ready for their use. Immediately the energy of the home changed, beckoning us to its call. The theatre's stage was set, familiar and primed for the healings' attendance once again.

Within minutes Donna and I found ourselves in the first room. Someone long held was straining to find their release and we both felt the urgency and willingness being emitted. Crossing the room, standing quietly side by side, we shielded and opened up to the call.

"Ouch," winced Donna, shifting her balance to her left leg. "My right leg kills me, does yours?" I stared nonplussed, my body was mirroring hers, so I was resting heavily on my right leg. The left throbbed but felt oddly numb too. Realization arrived simultaneously! This dear, elderly life had two amputated legs. We had clearly been given the registration of one each! "God bless these guides and the intelligence in our systems," I laughed. "Otherwise we'd both now be just face planted on the floor! Great 'Health and Safety at work' policy they have."

The persistent numbness and pain realigned our focus fast. "It's a gentleman," Donna nodded. "He's in a wheelchair and he's just going round and round the room. Bless him, he is desperate now to get out. Some of this is a projection of the record of those feelings he had when he was housebound. He became entrenched in the belief he would never get out, never escape."

As Donna had a strong clear visual and connection, it was natural for her to continue and assist him over whilst I focused my mind on holding the space. With clear intent for his safe passage onwards and all guiding hands present, Donna sank deeper into the process.

Time ticked by. The pains persisted. I stole a glance at Donna. Her face and stance were settled and deeply engaged. Clearly this gentleman was being accorded the respect and integrity of care to his departure too. As the mantel piece clock showed twenty minutes had passed, the energy in the room jolted and shifted. Blissful absence of pains and numbness returned and a familiar sense of update, recalibration, began to run through the auric record of the house. Stretching out her arms widely and rolling her shoulders, Donna nodded approvingly and opened her eyes.

"Been far?" I enquired, handing her some water. "It was a whole new learning again," said Donna as she flopped heavily into an armchair. His daughter came for him and she stood in a portal by the front door as he wanted to walk to her. But he had been in his wheelchair so long and without legs for so many years that his memory print was telling him he could not walk. The guides helped me to work with him to re-imagine his legs and see them again. It took some time but of course the ethereal blueprint was right there. However he then also wanted to dress in his suit and tie and meet his daughter proud and neat and upright. I held his arm to the front door and down the step and what a lovely reunion to see, with his daughter. So, another life is released! But crikey, I know how you felt now. That's absolutely drained me."

I fired some silver force into her wrists, projected colours into various accumulators and told her to take some time to allow the guiding hands to bring in all she needed. Meanwhile, feeling very energized and inspired, I busied myself cleaning and removing further any old residues that would prevent the house from becoming united in the present as one healthy happy whole again.

Less than an hour later, with brief explanations given and a full report promised to follow, we were back in the car, feeling content to have served another call. Yet the question remained between us both. Why the attention to the appearance in both of our experiences? It fascinated us to embed every learning, to really understand. As always, we trusted when the time was right the answers would arrive. And soon they did!

Part 3

A constant stream of clients found their way to the therapy centre and for some time I had been regularly treating a gentleman whom I trusted as a very gifted medium. During his next session I was suddenly urged to ask him if he could shed light on why some earthbound souls, who had missed their window initially, would find it so important to choose their attire and dress themselves when at last another window had been opened for them and was waiting with open arms. He immediately had an answer!

"They have often been buried in a shroud," he began. "It really does matter what you are dressed in. And some families are too upset to think about it, or to go through their loved ones' clothes so soon. Some do, and make choices their relatives do not like. Others, especially with cremation, may think it is a waste for expensive or decent clothes to go up in smoke. Both that lady and gentleman may well have just been buried in a hospital shroud or funeral home gown. It's a process of correction before they go over. And it's very needed for their settlement. They will have appreciated it immensely. And the healing guides beyond would know that, before they came over to truly help them to leave, it would be essential to allow. Then they would step into the next vibrational realm, waiting to welcome them as they envisaged or desired to."

It made perfect sense. I thought of the old pink dressing gown and hair net, and dearly hoped she had not been buried in her night wear with her hair pinned! The process of respect to each life and the closing ceremonies for the body, soul and spirit held a vast realm of questions of huge importance.

Thanking him deeply for his work and knowledge, and the two lives who had taught us so much, I lodged the learning deeply. Over a year later I discovered just how important that one piece of information was.

My drive to work took around 40 minutes through pleasant scenery which allowed time for projection into the day and to see what impressed itself upon me. After many years of training in practice each day, you become detached from your thoughts and feelings as a more thorough way of living, of being. An observer of what is registering in your systems and less 'involved' with whatever that is. It becomes necessary and natural to do so. Healing requires the holding of sacred space. A continual process of learning how to get oneself out of the way. The sanctuary of that alignment is the greatest safety and place of clear guidance you have.

Barely a few minutes into the commute on a sunny bright day, the vision of the lady in her pink dressing gown swam into view. Ten minutes later my thoughts were still revolving around the same theme. I searched my memory banks to see if it was the Anniversary of the date she had passed on from the house, but could not pin it down to that. So I simply observed the visual pictures and reminders, which persisted until the therapy room was prepared, and footsteps echoed on the stairs heralding the first client of the day.

Now, she happened to be an amazingly bright and capable lady I had treated since my earliest work in the charity healing room. Her effervescent spirit shone and she gave out a huge amount of herself in the support of others. Thus, a monthly session of recharge and cleansing of her aura and chakras as invaluable to her wellbeing.

That day she arrived, tears straining behind her eyes, usual composure gone as she threw her coat down carelessly. "I am so glad to be here today, Sue." No more words were possible, she broke. I scooped her up and just let her cry. No need for words, just hold a healing space.

What moves into that knows and will be greater and more powerful in those moments than any words or platitudes you can fill it up with. She shook for a while with tears and relief and had been ensconced in a chair and delivered the steaming mug of sweet tea before she spoke again.

"My Mum passed away two days ago, Sue. I have just felt sad, but barely cried at all until now, because it was such a beautiful assisted process. Never before have I seen the pure vitality of colours, the energies that power to hold and guide. It all was pure natural love. I helped her, helped all my family. Gave her healing throughout, sent out thanks for her life and for a safe passing to the next, and so much attended, so many came to accompany her onwards. Mum could see them, my brothers could sense them. I simply felt captivated by the serene power and strength of it and now left with a deep trust that's holding me together for everyone. Dad's left all the arrangements to me, so I will have to leave my phone on as there's so much to do.

But I knew I had to come here today."

Cupping her face in my hands, our eyes locked. The sparkle within hers was far greater than the grief that lay behind it. "You have just gifted your Mum the most profound true love anyone can proffer. To help someone so dear and serve their life journey with such strength and belief is a healing grace you contain and exude but never recognise in yourself. We'll help my love. Your Mum is so proud of you. And so grateful too. And it's no accident that you booked this day to be here over a month ago. Because all are also looking after your wellbeing."

A smile lit up her face. "You're right! I was compelled to not cancel and get here. They just know. And care for us so much." Whilst she composed herself, I went ahead to the healing room and mindfully dedicated a candle to the process of her Mum's passing. On entering the room her phone rang and I signalled for her to take all the time she needed. From the responses it was clear something had gone amiss. All the pent up emotions were brimming to the surface again.

"That was the undertaker," she gulped. "They have collected Mum, she's safely at the funeral home. But they haven't got the nightie. And they can't understand how it got lost." The sobs broke free. I looked to the sky and uttered a prayer of thanks. Now I would catch up with what the worlds beyond already knew and had been loading my systems with all the pictures and memories for. Passing a tissue I asked gently, "Why are you so upset about the nightie?" She dabbed her eyes, "Mum passed away in this pretty blue nightdress and she looked so serene and beautiful in it we all thought it would be lovely to bury her in it. So I asked the hospital to keep it safe and send it on with her so I could collect it and wash it for the undertakers to dress her in it. But somehow it's gone."

Intercepting her distress quickly I asked, "Did your Mum like outfits? Dress up for occasions? Take care with her appearance?" A little laugh escaped. "Oh my goodness, yes. She has three wardrobes. Adored outfits for special occasions and she always turned herself out very well, always."

"Ok," I replied, "so a nightdress wouldn't be her choice. And that's why she has made damn sure it's got lost. She has spent the morning making darn certain I know this!" As I explained, the clouds lifted and delight shone again in her face, incredulous at the linear intelligence and clarity. Concern suddenly elbowed its way back in. "But how will I know what outfit Mum wants to wear? Sue, how do I choose that for her?" I ushered her to the couch. "TRUST, you are so connected to her, she will tell us how. Now let's get some healing recharge into you. And down the wires to your family and your Mum."

For the next hour many healing energies moved in and out, rebalancing, clearing, bringing revitalizing peace. It never failed to amaze me how diligent and intently personal each healing session was for such busy realms to create. They led her into a deep meditative sleep inside of which I knew the pathways she would intuitively follow ahead were being laid and embedded into her receptive and trusting inner lives. Amidst it one message persistently made itself heard. I held it as the spark that would light the way and gently awoke her from the healing. She stretched happily like a cat. "I feel renewed, so much better. And I feel like I know. So I'm going straight to Mum and Dad's house to choose that outfit and take it to the undertakers.

Now I know it's all going to be as she wills. It's all going to be Okay."

"Excellent," I declared, "I have one piece of information that is key. It will guide and confirm your choice. Your Mum wants to be buried with a photograph from a memorable occasion, taken with the whole family together. That is what she has sent as the clue to help you. Ring me and let me know how you go." With parting hugs off she flew and I gathered myself quickly for the next client. Such a beautiful weave of timings and symmetry. A whole tapestry of threads and connections between us all, stretching to universes of intelligence. Another memorable moment lay just ahead for her, its sense nudging me, as I lit another candle for all that surrounded her to help her self-belief soar.

In a rare welcome gap between sessions, my phone rang. From the elation in her voice I knew the mission was accomplished and she was overjoyed. In total trust she had gone straight to the wardrobes. There was not a heartbeat of hesitation in pulling out an outfit that shone above all the rest. Emerald green suit in hand, she turned to take it over to the window and hang it in the daylight to study it closer. And as she did her eyes fell on the photograph there, with pride of place in the bedroom. Picking it up, her Mum's energy encircled her as she gazed at the happiness on all their faces. A beautiful holiday all together in Ireland. And there in the centre, Dad grinning from ear to ear with Mum beaming next to him, and the whole family around them. Bright and resplendent in that very emerald green suit.

Together there is no circle we cannot complete. With the truth and magic of what we are joined, with all we are of, there is no journey we cannot unite around. And the grace of that unification, is the beating Heart at the centre of every universe. The pulsing eternal issue of unconditional love that will carry us gently home when the time comes.

Chapter 11

Expanding Sensory Dimensions and Remote Viewing

I t was the last healing session of the day where the familiar frequency of the day settled into the dusk and evening emanations. Tangibly so different to the forces bringing in the morning or heralding the afternoon. The rhythm of years of working had printed a memory stick within me, recording the specific notes and flavours of each day and the particular unique atmosphere resonances of each month.

Blissfully asleep, this young life before me had already been touched by many events and 'life shocks' but she had protection around her that was tangibly strong. My work was scrutinized as layers of trauma were peeled away and energetic wounds were bathed and barmed. Balancing waves of green force arrived accompanied by the purifying serenity of violet. The white walls turned green with the banks of energy dancing around the room. Interspersing them, the pattern of the clear slanted lines' pure violet travelled in, producing a feast for the electrical vision of the eyes. Yet, for all I could witness, how much more did I not see, hear, smell, touch and taste with the entirety of the senses?

As the thought drifted through, the source of protection suddenly came into view. A tall silver and pale blue figure standing by the young lady's left shoulder. Stock still and strong, it emanated protection with the sharpness of flint. Yet, a certain gentle courtesy too. Very slowly I raised my head, eyes travelling up the steely rigid exterior, clarity dawning of why the essence of absolute safety I felt accompanying her at each healing was so powerful. The Knight's face was not visible through the closed helmet, but I sensed he might be smiling just a little. His standard was held out parallel to his right side and what physically would have been such heavy medieval silver grey armour simply radiated lightness through the pale blue frequency he was a part of.

I bowed my head to him in greeting. He remained unmoving, on duty and in service to his realm. What a perfect presence of safety they had sent to walk alongside this life! Many questions arose, but the mind softly swept them aside. Neither was an inquiry from me appropriate, nor did the Knight's demeanour suggest conversation featured on his duty rota! Emitting gratitude to him I sealed the process.

However, as usual there were further reasons to being shown glimpses of this ethereal realm of security, for as the energy was elevated in intensity and purity, so too did the depths of severity of what it exposed. Like a high-powered laser it penetrated deeper and once the search beam of light homed in what surfaced was a broad graded scale of forces. From the residual waste static that's all part and parcel of daily process and exchange, to the denser, hotter and stickier residues of the more 'unpleasant' happenings in life. For every 7 seconds our systems exhaust into our aura, leaving the sequins of prints of every experienced moment within the memory banks of the auric sheath. Connected by millions of tiny threads to cells within the organs and tissues of the body, our iron rich blood is not only a carrier, but also a tape recorder of events. We each are a unique physical and energetic library of every facet of this present living experience. And the capacity for connections to more of our soul's experiences, to past lives, talents, knowledge and innate skills are all there ready. All await to tell their stories and the calls and needs of this incarnation now, and seek healing they may need too.

But, there are also the dark zones. The places where first even Angels do not tread. The areas where those dragon energies, which remain uncorrupted and free to serve higher purpose, will enter ahead to cleanse and clear. Making safe the arena for the High to move into. For coarse force will feed from finer. Will destroy the High. Those dragon forces are a platoon of knights to the realms of Ascended Masters and of Angels. They are the foot soldiers who pave the way for safe entry. All strata have their Agencies of Protection and Security.

So, as the attending healing powers rose in finesse and potency, so too did the temperature ever decrease as the higher the force, the colder it is. Icy fingers and hands had become customary, but now pure wool cardigans became necessary to manage certain healings, and clients were swathed in layers of cotton and wool blankets. Never synthetics, for static emissions will stick to such fabrics, cooking you and the recipient in a toxic trap of exhaust and waste. Rendering the purifying process null and void.

With every elevation of energy, standards, and attention to every detail had to rise with it. A whole new level of transmutation was ripening, ready to burst onto the scene. Dark and light can be misrepresented with language such as bad and good.

Sweeping judgments that are wholly inaccurate. In our world where we measure all by comparisons; i.e. the drink in this glass is cold, whilst this beverage without ice is warmer, without darkness we could not identify that light exists at all!

Thus coarser and finer becomes a better reference scale for energy. And the dark has its finer within range, just as the light has a grading of finesse within it too. Accordingly, the quality of our process in thoughts, feelings, actions and deeds, will determine the level of finesse of our auras. Within that there will be more fixed, permanent radiations, from well-trodden pathways of actions and deeds and thoughts, which all create multitudes of different forms, shapes and colours in varying positions in the auric field. And then there are the present emissions constantly into the aura, which in colour will shine from pale pastel shades to darker. As human beings we will move through the colour chart all the time. It's neither practical, nor expected, amidst day to day 'wear and tear' that we exhaust the palest pastel radiations constantly.

Anyway, some strident colour is often needed! And apt too! So, yes, at times we will have 'colourful language' as we are far too multi-faceted, if truly engaged in life, to be 'beige'.

Alongside what we personally cause and create in our radiation, there is also, of course, what others around us cause. Without any judgments, all of us have at some point, taken a seat on a bus or train next to someone and alighted at our journey's end either feeling somewhat more energized, or drained. We are processing machines, and between us there is a continual exchange. There are friends and family members we naturally migrate to where all mutually enjoy the sensations of feeling uplifted, happier, more settled and just better all round for that company.

And we know the contrast, where a kind of 'mood hoovering' experience occurs and we are left feeling drained of power, with sludge in the tank! The natural flow is that the brighter will enhance those resonating less so, and this applies to the radiation of our physical well-being as well as the quality of the mental and emotional process. It is an eternal 'new shiny lit up lamps for old lamps' process of exchange in every moment, situation and interaction.

As a healer it is imperative to understand this natural process. To know how to create ecologies that will minimize the containment of exhausts and attract the higher and finer forces too. Ways to cleanse and maintain both the ecology of healing space and one's own systems. Because, you are signing each day an ethereal contract to work with, and be an agency for rare and pristine realms. To honour them as an exacting portal through which they can travel. The sheer rate of process from each 'end of the bar' as the central pivot between them and the client, is demanding. For you enter a veritable circus of impressions in every single treatment you do. A bombardment of varying degrees of energies. Some will call to be opened, explored, forgiven, understood in order to relegate them. Others will never become conscious, dealt with by compassionate intelligence. Important to know when to dive deep, when to paddle shallow. Imperative to know always when to stay neutral, impersonal, detached.

Acutely timed empathy is the healer's lightning rod, to detract the shocks of storms and hold the ecology for peace to enter. Sympathy however will eat you up one bite at a time in powered processes. Thus you become an acrobat in the circus, a lion tamer in the ring and you learn to spot the clowns and avoid them like feedback of a badly baked sponge at the Women's Institute Fair.

By now it's freefall down the rabbit hole! No desire to even find a foothold, just let in the eternal drive of falling in love with the Mystery. How can we fall further and get joyfully lost deeper, whilst at the same time be ever more secure in knowing throughout that we are found? The beauty of polarities is so!

Inner lives are now all honed. Nerves, muscles, organs, endocrine system, brain and heart pathways and more, continually reading the ever-expanding bandwidth of reception through sight, touch, taste, hearing and smell. Through them the previously invisible worlds begin to happen. Often it begins so enticingly in the peripheral vision, but when you turn to look square on nothing appears to be there. With practice, you learn to soften your gaze, begin to see the etheric glow, the innermost strata of the aura.

Every living organism radiates, so soon the emanation around trees, plants, birds and animals becomes part of normal sight. High humidity in the air makes it easier to see these forces. As can the potency and light of dawn and dusk. The first time you see a complete aura your life changes. Observing the entire 'disappearance' of the physical body and in its place the vitality of the energetic bubble we live within. Set to its eternal 7 second refresh rate, the cascading light show is mesmerizing. So vivid and very obviously real, one emerges from the 'show' totally stupefied that you have lived unaware of this profound personal space stretching feet beyond where your body finishes. And how, with millions of encounters with fellow human souls, have you failed to realize they too function inside of a lightshow? It's completely incomprehensible once seen, experienced and inside of your living range of reference. Like dancing all night and totally missing the shiny disco ball at the centre of the floor!

This is when the tumble down the rabbit hole escalates. Because around every bend your breath is bated with anticipation. Arms and legs are now flailing, eager to keep up the momentum of free fall. For the brain has soon lobbed in a thought bomb, a question that lands mesmerizingly hissing like a landmine. What else am I not seeing? How much have I so far missed in this sleepwalk through life? Have I seriously just kept my sleep mask on the whole bloody journey?

Every opportunity is seized to soften the gaze and reconnect with the vision within this magical realm of purity of colour, shapes and forms. As third eye vision escalates in its activation too, the mind seizes the joys of ever-expanding fields of impressions and the brain learns to be present to the experiences, acutely storing the sequins of the moments without continually trying to reference and understand at the point. Now everything has joined the party, dancing in synchronicity and revelling in this feast the senses serve.

Those senses are now training like a seasoned five a side team. Rejoicing in being taken from the sidelines, they are keenly engaged in play in the arena of life. Finding positions, they hone their interplay, revelling in the pursuit of new skills, together a well-oiled machine. Touch becomes ever more attuned to feeling the finer. Whilst the subtleties of blockages, static residues, the radiation from different organs, bones and nerves, buildings and lands, become a natural part of the hands and the very skin's reality, hearing dials up the volume, tuning in to changes in pitch and frequency, so life always has a background soundtrack. From the pure deafening bliss of peace to the gentle tones of serenity. Or the invasive annoyance of electricity running around the wiring in the walls. Normality becomes always hearing the previously unheard.

And then there are the messages, the guidance, wisdoms which are a whole other level of mystery. Where the issuing sources seem to be sitting so close in on your shoulder that the ear, or ears seem to receive and transmit internally all at the same time. It's like they actually bounce the words around not only the inside of your head, but throughout your whole being because everything gets the message. Enhanced hearing moves into some mysterious realm of thorough absorption where 'I'm All ears' truly does take on a meaning for real!

When not to be left out, the sense of smell heightens, there is not only the balancing act of adapting in situations to what at first seems sensory overload, but also at times you want to lodge a complaint against your nose for assault and battery!

Because it is one thing to pick up a melon and take in the sweet vapours of its vital force like never before. Or suddenly smell the ethereal wafts of a favourite fragrance that announces the close presence of a loved one. It is entirely another to be assailed by the aroma of what certain emotions emit, or the memory prints that unsavoury life events leave behind.

When they get exposed, flushed out of hiding, by healing emanations it can be the less pleasant point of waking up your faculties! But what about when the sensory worlds of smell actually evidence the living active connections between human lives? Enter stage left, the day it chose to begin to show me itself as a dynamic of evocation. A mistress of wonder in its own right.

The cascade of events began with a client who had a difficult relationship with his Father. He was keen for it to improve, so after some facing of truths and ownership of his part to play, I began focusing on the connections between them both. The visual pictures were extremely clear and the healing flowed and fizzed up and down the wires and mutual threads. He began to sniff. I joined in, rather bemused. Where was this aroma of cooking coming from? By then we were a duo of ever more rapid sniffs.

Seconds later he shot off the couch inhaling the air like a tracker dog pursuing a kilo of heroin! "That," he announced incredulously, "is my dad's chicken casserole! It's my favourite dish he cooks. I would know that aroma anywhere!" I blinked incredulously too. This was a whole new departure altogether. "Well," I began slowly, "The healing was flowing along the connection between you. And I guess food and cooking is a big way many people express and share their love. Maybe this is the only medium through which he can and does."

He was nodding vigorously and donning his coat. "I'll ring you when I get home and tell you if Dad has been cooking that casserole whilst I was here with you." And off he shot! Along with Donna who was also running out of the door at a highly unusual rate of knots. I sniffed the hallway. The fragrance of chicken hung in the air. Mystified, I began to chime out the corners and incense. The next client was expecting a treatment, not a pub lunch!

Forty minutes later my phone rang, excitement rippled in his voice. "I really feel that's opened up some real clarity between us, Sue. 25 miles to home and I just felt so much lighter. And I walked through the door to smiles from Dad. And chicken casserole is just ready on the stove. He said he was really thinking deeply about me and felt compelled to make it, to show he cares. Just telling him of the experience has brought us closer together."

We both sent our gratitude to the wonders of healing reconciliation and ended our call in mutual amazement. The sound of Donna's feet on the stairs were rapid. Had she connected into the force behind Ferrari today? "Oh, I'm so glad you've incensed," she puffed, flicking on the kettle. "Where did that incredible smell of chicken casserole come from? My whole room filled up with it and in the hallway it was so strong. I let my client out and I had to run to get lunch. It made me ravenous. But where did it come from?"

As I explained, her expression mirrored my incredulity. No words were needed between us. We knew the signs pointed to another elevation. A brand spanking new classroom of teaching and learning. And as Donna's client had also hot footed it to the bakery for lunch, her stomach growling from the anticipation of food the cooking aromas had caused, we were very happy indeed. Four witnesses to the same phenomena were in our incredible world, a very helpful and welcome gift! Little time passed before this sensory arena pulled us further over the threshold of its theatre and manifestation.

Independently of each other, Donna and I had been regularly smelling cigarette smoke along the hallway and on the stairs. Eventually, one evening, we both completed our last session at the same time and I opened my door to Donna muttering away about the lingering smell of cigarette smoke. AGAIN! It was particularly strong. Realizing neither of us had confided this to the other before, we put our heads together, both holding the same views. Our dear 'night watchman' smoked on duty! Joking that perhaps he ought to stub it out, or take a crafty smoke break in the loo, we cleaned up and left for the night.

A few mornings later I breezed in, did the morning preparations and opened the loo door, to be greeted by a very strong odour. Not smoke this time, but the tangible smell a cigarette has when it has been stubbed out. I sniffed around like the old Bisto Kid advert trying to trace the source. Around the washbasin was particularly whiffy! Absorbed in being Sherlock, for nothing captures every faculty like a good old mystery, I inhaled deeply. The mirror, it was definitely most pungent by the mirror. Carefully I lifted the bottom edge away from the wall. And lo, balanced neatly on the ledge behind the mirror was a freshly stubbed out cigarette!

As I exited the toilet, Donna arrived. It did look suspiciously like I was the culprit! But then we recalled exactly what we had said and in fairness our bluff had royally been called! A cigarette break seemed to have been had in the loo! Examining the tailor-made cigarette, we were further mystified to find even the brand was old. Neither of us could recall seeing them on the shelves for years. How could our watchman presence not only have the ability to manifest that, but also the wit to secrete it behind the mirror? This was a pretty freaky occurrence even for us.

At this time, in healings, the physical and energy worlds merged like never before. It became akin to being within a continual portal of appearance and relegation and the power was amping up. Light bulbs were popping daily and the flow was seamless. It was building to something big. The crescendo certainly went with a bang.

Having a little time before the final client of the day was due, I cleaned and tidied the kitchen and toilets and had just swept and washed the stairs when she arrived. A vibrant lady, well- tuned in to energy and vibration, she was soon relaxing on the couch and a blissful session was well in progress.

The force went up. We glanced at each other surprised by its power. It continued to climb and with each surge the lamp dimmed and then brightened again. My systems linked to the sense and memory of a previous experience that had felt exactly the same. The dimming and brightening of the lamp escalated along with the intensity of force. That former time, when the lights had gone this crazy, the healing forces were working on clearing some very dark astral light prints.

It was many years before, when Donna's healing appointments were regularly 'hijacked' by an intended purpose or need for cleansing and rebalance in numerous locations on earth. We were carried along with it as willing recruits. However, on that occasion we stumbled into bringing our own intention into the process. It was a steep learning curve amidst a far too huge and ambitious try.

We were 'rescued' after scaring the pants off ourselves and given a thorough reprimand. Our guidance was very clear. "Learn this lesson well or your licence will be revoked!" All the learning had been embedded thoroughly. To listen well and work within the parameters and purpose they gave. Never, ever again to lead the very best friends we work with and for, into dangerous territory. And forgiveness followed swiftly as they read our radiation rise to their standard. Later, I was assured that they could have stopped us sooner. But a lesson learned the hard way is the best way of all to find the limits and never cross them again.

I had no idea what was afoot in the locality, or even further afield. It was clear through the power pack of our clean ecology and I had been enrolled into lessening or preventing some crime or harm. My client was remaining remarkably calm but was very aware. There was far more healing presence than needed. With as simple and brief an explanation as possible, I asked her to just trust me and put my full concentration into it. The atmosphere held an intense chill. Ice sculpture cold, my systems felt razor sharp. Then bang! The lamp surged to brilliance and blew. Click, the fuses tripped out. Total darkness descended and enveloped us.

Trying to find words of reassurance I looked out of the window. All the street lights were out. The traffic lights too. "What the heck happened, Sue?" Lighting some candles to gather composure, all I could truthfully say was that the sheer volume of force that had attended whatever mission they were on had wiped out the power in the local area. Knowing it was futile I clicked the switches in the fuse box on, glad of the many candles and torches we had to hand.

After giving the client some settlement, she left, still quite stunned but gladly knowing this was not 'usual' service. As I turned to climb the stairs, there on a step lay another identical half cigarette. The stairs had been swept and washed less than two hours previously and the door was always locked when the last client arrived. Picking it up, the sense of total security coursed through me. Our watchman had really been working hard to protect us that night and he wanted me to know. The strangeness continued and, being 'alone' in the shadowy darkness of the centre, when next an old alarm system, long disabled, suddenly began to ring, my nerves almost gave out. With no code to quieten its shrieking bells, I fetched my mobile to ring the landlord. For the first time ever, not one bar, absolutely no signal! Just outside the building was a telephone kiosk, so I locked the door and scurried in there. The telephone was dead. What level of force takes out power and phone signals and wires? And activates a deactivated alarm? It had never rung before when the power had been cut off to fit new lights, so could not be some latent back up system.

By now I was very sure those fire dragons had been very hard at work preventing some atrocity. And me turning to jelly was not going to cut it! So, with the air of a woman with a degree in electronics, I rammed the step ladder under the alarm box, climbed it with an exaggerated huff and numerous expletives and brandished my scissors. There were three wires. Great! "Thank God this is not bomb disposal," I muttered, "at worst I'll get a shock, get chucked off the ladder! Come on guys, which colour? Green, red or black?" The silence was deafening and the irrational effect of feeling severely pissed off took over. My scissors opened and cut through all three! Alarm bells seized and my legs wobbled on the step ladder.

Bewildered by the sudden total calm and wondering if one day I would just get blown up by the force or fried to a crisp, my feet decided they were heading out the door fast. Medicinal brandy was calling me!

The next morning there was a long queue into town. Temporary traffic lights bordering a large hole in the road. Men in yellow jackets busily mending cables. Light met me as I opened the door. Our power was restored. When Donna arrived she stared at the matching cigarette butts as the previous night's events were recounted. Knowing that much energy could be routed through our centre and take out the district's power was extreme to our well-seasoned minds.

But what had been happening? We scoured the local papers but could find no crimes or harms perpetrated that stood out beyond the usual. Either it was much farther away, or something had been averted. So often we knew at the point, or after, but silence remained about this event.

After replacing numerous blown light bulbs and giving the entire centre a thorough electrical cleanse, we shielded it extra strongly with gold force around the outside, and pale blue inside. All realms that ensured our safety were thanked, especially the watchman. We never smelled cigarette smoke again. However, the phenomenon was not yet over. The Master Teachers just nodded their approval by taking us into the next level of our sensory crash course!

It was part way through a gentle tranquil treatment. On the couch, calm and serene, lay a very pure and spiritual lady. Healing was flowing down the clear lines of connection, to and from her Mother. Then everything flipped into a different dimension, where time speeded up, so that all occurring happened in slow motion. A glorious smell of Asian spices and cooking rose in the air. This time I knew it was permeating the entire centre with its wonderful tantalizing aroma.

At the same time as the lady sat bolt upright declaring, "That's my Mum's Tarka Dhal. I would know it anywhere." I found myself in her Mum's kitchen!

Now this was a new experience yet again. Yes, I had experienced remote viewing in distance healing work, but this was different. And certainly, never in an actual hands-on session whilst simultaneously smelling delightful Asian home cooking. I stared astonished at the back of her Mum, who was standing at her stove stirring a pan which emitted vapours that made my stomach growl. The stirring slowed as her energy bodies sensed mine. Turning, with spoon in hand, she faced me with an amused half smile. "Not in my kitchen!" she shouted, "not while I am cooking."

With each word the wooden implement was waved fiercely, but comically in my direction. Seemingly, my energy bodies did not need telling twice. So the next second I was back in the treatment room. For another few seconds we just stared at each other incredulously and then she broke the spell. "What's going on, Sue? THAT is my Mum's Tarka Dhal. First I smelled the onions and now the whole dish is getting stronger. How can that be?" My eyes felt like they were spinning. How the heck had I now turned into some space cadet that could defy matter and physicality and merge with that ecology in every way? And how the heck did I explain this one?

"Well," I began slowly, "quite how I am not sure, but I just found myself transported to your Mum's kitchen. And I can confirm she is stirring a pan, the contents of which smell exactly the same as this room! She sensed me there, turned and waved her wooden spoon at me and told me, 'Not in my kitchen. Not while I am cooking'. Now to be fair, it is highly unusual, and somewhat rude of me, to just pop in like that, so I would have thrown myself out too! In my defence, you are clearly on her mind and the connections between you both are incredible."

She blinked fast and reached for her phone. "I'm ringing Mum," and hit the number decisively. Meanwhile I did a quick check and duly found the group working in the workshop room were all feeling extremely hungry and mystified by the spicy aromas. Explanation, if at all possible, would have to wait. Donna and I passed in the hallway, a quizzical look on her face as she hastily pulled on her coat. "I'll explain later," I promised. "And maybe work out how to stop this," she shot back, "before we are both breaking the scales!" She was right, my stomach was growling with hunger pangs too.

Returning to the room, the call ended and our eyes met. "You're right, Sue. She is at the stove cooking. And I am right too, it's Tarka Dhal. That is absolutely incredible. But how, how can the smell appear here? And how can you arrive there?" As I sat down preparing to try to piece it all together, a question had to be asked. "How far have those aromas travelled and how far did I go?" "Birmingham," she smiled. "It's quite some distance in a few seconds." So, already, I inwardly mused, the energies have doubled the distance! I silently prayed no one from Australia would book in. Surely even a space cadet would get travel sick pulling that off!

As we sat together and talked, I realized that as the sense of smell is connected into the emotions, in both incidents it had been a joining of the emotional energy bodies. Also, each parent was not only thinking about their son, or daughter, they were cooking food that was most special to them. Each time, the energy body of their emotions had met beyond all physical material world limitations. Where distance and time does not feature and scent can manifest within that dimension. Just as so many testify to smelling a favourite fragrance of a loved one who has passed away. They announce their presence through that familiar scent as they move into the vibrational dimension we inhabit. For good measure, the mental body, which is connected to the sense of sight, had 'hitched a lift' in the second experience. I am sure the higher senses had quite a jolly together that day! And brought food to the party too!

It transpired that the wise higher realms had good reason to connect us so strongly that day as there was much more to come. Regularly the antennas on those pathways would call my attention to distance healing and it naturally flowed to both Mum and Daughter. Some weeks passed before suddenly I found myself once again next to her Mum. But this time we had both travelled… into the kitchen of the healing centre in the early hours of the morning. I was tucked up in bed having this 'waking dream' which was clear and vivid in every detail when my physicality awoke.

Our discussion was deep and the Mother's concern was palpable. True healing guides had called on me and brought us together because her worry and anxiety travelling to her daughter was not helping her at all. And that morning a very important appointment lay ahead. It was vital to settle this before that time. So amidst very powerful rays of energy, which were amplified in that vibrational field we had met in, a whole therapeutic conversation passed between us. It ended with me counselling that she now needed to go into a deep sleep, and trust everything was going to be fine.

Later that day I answered my phone to a very happy voice telling me that an important appointment had gone amazingly and she was bursting to share her news. Indeed it had been early that morning and the addition of her Mum worrying was travelling down the wires constantly. But, there had been a blessed absence of it to carry that day and on calling her Mother with the positive news, a most unusual thing had happened. I began to laugh. She paused,

"You know Sue, don't you?" she asked. I said, "I think you are going to say she slept through the entire morning."

"Oh my God Sue, yes. It's unheard of, she slept deeply until midday! What did you do?" It was very moving to explain what had occurred and wonder together at the sheer love and attendance of the healing realms. Such deep love, trust and spirituality between them both. And what an honour to be allowed into those sacred threads of connection. The special bonds between a beautiful Mother and Daughter.

Later I sat quietly basking in the many moments these vast sensory networks had gifted. The rich pure colours that electrical vision opened life up to. The extraordinary finesse touch enabled as the inner lives registered the external worlds. Healing hands devoted to remedy power of rebalance and cure, coursing through the fingertips. Palms that detect blockages and static residues and clear them away. Hearing that receives and transmits, tuned to frequencies, vibrations bringing guidance and knowledge.

The miracle of the sense of smell, the emotional life's window into the world. Yes, this is their world, that latter realm had manifested the most tangible and extraordinary moments. Broken through into new dimensions. Proved there are no boundaries or divisions or separations.

We all are of energy and of Source, simply vibrating at different frequencies according to where in the journey of lives we are.

But most of all, it demonstrated the Power of Love.

Chapter 12

Lessons From Darkness and Light

Echoes of Past Lives

Part 1

E xactly the same as gym training, by the seventh year of intensive healing work, they had built my physical and spiritual processing muscles up to often managing an eighty-hour week. With regular treatments for myself and attention to maintaining my aura and a consistently clean ecology, the sheer amperage and volume of force passing through me kept me steadfastly answering to the needs and calls they brought in.

My personal trainers were rigorous, but very generous with their help. The rewards were vast in witnessing client's lives improve through clean-up, rebalancing and counsel. A thorough approach equipping each with the tools to enable that transformation through their own volition and appreciation to development and change. In between those joyous triumphs however, the many harrowing hardships and harms revealed, make for delicate work. For once a life has trusted and placed themselves in your hands, the contract is sealed to provide every protection and aid you can to alter the course and trajectory it's been on.

Changing their life, only the person can do for themselves. But we cannot create new with old patterns and habits. And sure footedness ahead requires fresh earth that has been tilled of the past hurts and wounds. So that a firm foundation can be assembled brick by brick to ensure the stability for the present and the future.

Such intimate disclosures, so often of deep traumas and harms never spoken of before, which lie embedded at the core of physical and mental illnesses, addictions and life limiting patterns, charges the healer with the holding in secure confidence and person's deepest wounds and fears. Summoning every sinew to protection and remedy at each level has one rooting through the tool kit of life changing ways and means, so they can be handed over and tried towards success and overcoming. Those who pick them up and apply them become the change they seek. And greater architects of their own destiny. Just as the source of human life decreed.

Forever in the wings, all that guides and heals is watchful of their charge's own well-being throughout. The health of a clear balanced channel is vital. Never will they give anyone more than they can handle. But we will be stretched. And we will be tested too. For resistance and overcoming is how we grow and evolve.

Of course, I will never know at which of their particular 'board meetings' the 'Council of Elders and Guides' decided that my endurance on the treadmill had been established. Balance on the yoga ball was now acceptable. And stamina on the cross trainer had been proven!

Steadfastness amidst uncertain and demanding situations had been given a big universal tick. Thus the motion, in my conscious absence, was passed to move me onto weights!

Did they toss me a couple of dumbbells? No! As per usual Sue's resume clearly must have been embellished in red ink, maybe many lives ago, who knows? With the comment, "Got promising instincts .... Likely to catch a cannon ball if lobbed at her!"

So, yep, the heavy weights just found their own sweet way onto the bar. And then the 'board' retired to observe, to see if I fell over, or handed in my notice by running, screaming, out of the door. As somewhere in my aura glistens a wilful sequin, emblazoned with a neon sign, flashing "I am no quitter," when a particularly sinister, dark presence materialized early on in this healing. I invariably did none of the above and cracked on!

The client I knew very well from many previous sessions, spanning some years, to ever improving effects. However, turbulence and upset had left her drained and anxious. Her steady reasoned hand on the tiller has smoothed and barmed the storms selflessly but had cost her dearly.

Adrenaline and fear were coursing through her constantly and none of her usual practices in self-mastery were maintaining her. I already had an inkling that something within the same resonances of the experience had stirred the pot deeper in her soul. Hints of past life trauma were surfacing and flashing through my mind's eye. And her fine-tuned intuition was picking up on them too.

The dark form continued to hover in the doorway. Satisfied that the force field of light present contained it at the threshold, I stole a sideways glance. Shocked, my eyes travelled up the long black robe to her head covering. A nun! She exuded misery and loathing, which at first I thought was about herself. I quickly realized its focus was transmitted upon the lady, quivering and upset on the couch. The touch paper of absolute intent to resolve and remove was lit like a firecracker and I followed its blazing trail deeper into the task. The visual cues and clues had to have my absolute concentration. Maybe the nun would get dealt with along the way.

Balming swathes of pale yellow wrapped itself around us. Pastel shades of lime green emitted from my fingertips. Placing my right hand over my solar plexus, the balancing equilibrium ran through the nervous system. She opened her eyes.

"Sue, I am being taken through memories of being at school. I had terrible panic attacks as a child. I had to go to a convent school and the nuns scared me. They were all dressed so darkly and some were so harsh." Ushering her to keep following the thoughts and allow them, I assured her that they were surfacing to be resolved. For never do the Higher Realms allow anything without pure focus to good reason and remedy. We pressed on. By now the visuals were showing me another life print and in this incarnation she had been a nun.

I knew, for her, this life of service was a calling she had embraced with passion and joy. Her love of selfless acts of compassion for others, purely an expression of her nature. And I realized this had spanned more than one lifetime. No wonder being in the modern world was so overwhelming for her. The safety and sanctity of the nunnery had been her blessing then. But different life paths had been chosen, to stretch her capacities anew, and for certain bring remedy for some deep woundings amidst these soul life experiences.

Beginning to work with Emotional Freedom Technique (EFT) which taps gently on key points of the meridians, helping the inner lives and cellular memories to locate the roots of their traumas locked within different organs, and bring them to the fore, a sudden quick movie played through my mind's eye. The thread I had been pulling on was mentally transmitting to her inner intelligence to lead us to when they had helped another person and it had caused them deep distress.

For this was the trace of the present, in this life now experience, which had evoked this extremis of fear reactions. Out of hardships and pain, all that loves us will always open up the opportunity to create positive change and correction. The dark presence fitted in somehow, in its chance of release, of purification I hoped! But, later for her, because this 'movie' was playing at speed.

A war plane, clear in my vision, falling from the sky. I could even hear the sounds as its engine sputtered and stopped. The eerie silence of it hurtling fast to the ground, crashing into a field, mangled and crushed. The propeller uselessly spinning from impact. And there running towards the plane was a mass of black robes. Many nuns calling to each other as they hurtled as one towards the plane. Flames licked hungrily from the wreckage bringing the nuns to a stop. All except one. She ran on, straight to the door, pulling and screaming for help, to get the pilot out. The heat was burning the flesh of her hands. Flames were spreading, catching her clothing. And then she was dragged, kicking and screaming away. Rolled and rolled on the grass to extinguish her smoking robe. Half dragged, half pushed. Propelled away from the burning wreckage before it exploded. Before it consumed her too.

The explosion had just erupted as the lady sat bolt upright. "Sue, can you smell smoke?" Reassuring her there was no physical fire, and we were amidst some of the roots of the fear and anxiety, she settled back down. It is a cautious journey, when a person's soul record and systems have released such a trauma from the unconscious. Unwise to rush in and explain it, for that thus reloads it into the conscious mind. However, if it becomes evident that the person is within the trace of the revelation, then it is intended as useful within the healing process.

Whatever the case, your task is to bring all to safe completion and hold the required confidentiality between those inner lives, the higher and yourself.

Equally, afterwards in your own download of the day and sealing of the work established, you work through emotions you have about it. Out to resolve and clean completion. For otherwise you carry residual energy which is not yours to hold onto. Everything radiates and in the respect to the life who has been brave enough to access that memory trauma and release it, you honour their life path and place it unattached and clear in your value system as another grace of service allowed and enabled. Another life who has trusted in you. In return you continue to earn all trust by the cleanest of dealings and closure.

In this instance however, the trace of memories she had been led to were quite astonishing. This informed me that, right from a child, echoes of some past life events had always been close to the surface. And had been intrinsic to the panic attacks and anxieties brought through and into the present incarnation. Her account was so clear of how one day in class she heard a plane overhead. A surge of fear coursed through her and she totally panicked. Fleeing from the classroom, the teacher shouting after her, she ran and ran, seeking somewhere to hide. All she could sense was this overwhelming surety that the plane was going to fall from the sky!

As I worked on, every healing method graced, to completely clear the deep trauma, it became clear that an explanation in this case was correct. Her memory had naturally been taken to the places where greater understanding lay. And to know that a background fear and panic that had echoed throughout her life to date had been imprinted so deeply due to past trauma, and in this case, a most heroic act, was only right to impart.

Deeper than the physical wounds and pain, how severe had her sorrow been at the loss she had witnessed? No wonder her call to 'rescue', to step in, and be compelled to 'save lives' so often at cost to herself, had always governed her so hugely.

She was amazed at the timing and clarity of the smell of the smoke. But most of all hugely relieved to finally know this was not blind unwarranted panic. Her sensitivity as a child was so acute to her surroundings. And her reactions to the plane were totally reasonable. There had been no attempts to comfort her from the nuns ever. But the deep balm that truth and understanding brings soon filled all those spaces in the child within and fizzed along every wiring pathway of the nerves. As the relief embraced her I moved further out in the aura to clear and settle each layer. And suddenly bumped into a stumming dark bank of force. "Ah crap," I inwardly murmured, "forgot about the Nun!"

Two insights ricochet through simultaneously. First the presence was telling me of another layer. Of another previous life event awaiting clearing. The second akin to the fuel tank warning flashing on your dashboard. Today was not the time to tackle this. Neither of us had the needed gas in our reserves to do this. Plus, a sense of calm and greater easement had been won. 'Enough' the signals all flashed for one day.

Working on, I began to transmit to the Nun. She stood unmoving, impenetrable, just sinisterly exuding a presence that repelled every attempt to penetrate towards resolve. What had made a heart turn to stone? How had lesser force removed her from the promise of what was possible to aspire to, and consumed her? To become so lost in negative unpleasant emotions?

Onwards I tried. No portal appeared. Nothing familiar I could follow. I ran through love, forgiveness, and kindness. None had legs. They would not walk, flow towards a force that would consume them, diminish them too. Worse, my client's awareness had picked up on the presence. I had to find a way before anxiety surged again. Fear, of all the emotions, feeds such force the most powerfully of all.

Returning to her side, I carefully chose my words. That we had another layer to heal and be explained deeper, but not today. And I needed to focus completely on closing this process, it was just taking a while to do. In trust's hands she settled down again. My mind was now picking at a thread of thought.

Early on in my initial training I had been led to a very wise teacher. Always she had given exactly the right guidance, in specific insights and wording I needed. And at the very time required too. Recently she had recommended a book, which had fascinated me, of healing methodologies developed and passed down over lifetimes and generations within peoples still living endemic natural lives upon earth.

A particular chapter was now uppermost on my radar. It explained how lower entities could attach themselves to people, draining their energy and causing numerous disruptions. The need was to locate the chakra, or chakras they were attached through. However this could potentially be very new terrain for me. For I tread a foot wrong and it could arc and connect into me. There was an instant chorus in my ears to immediately close the door on that thought pathway. Never enter with an open resonance that is pitching for the very thing you do not want!

I slammed the door and locked and bolted it tight! The ways had to be within me then. That's all I knew. Knowing had never failed me yet!

Carefully, I sensed each of her chakras. The throat for sure! Scanning my coloured silks, violet pitched clear and strong above all other frequencies. I laid it gently over her throat chakra.

Transmutation through violet was very powerful - one previous extreme experience with the realm of violet had shown its power to the maximum.

My attention returned to the Nun. Energy was building, whistling in my ears, laser like through the crown of my head. Suddenly all the reaching for forgiveness, love, kindness just melted away. No judgment. No feelings at all. Neutrality about whatever darkness had taken ownership and consumed many a sacred chance at life. A gritty lump within my core grew to flint. Clear, tough, equally impenetrable, it spoke, "No more of others' stains shall be upon this life's soul." The darkness glowered. My skin crawled.

Spine ramrod straight, I looked at the entity square on. Two words shot from my mind with such velocity it felt like the room shook. "Fuck off." And she did. Before my eyes she was gone!. Transmuted and removed just like that! They were bang on right. I certainly did have the ways within me! How many occasions had they witnessed my colourful grasp of the English language? The violet ray will banish that which cannot be salvaged. Render unto Caesar that which is his due. Insights were playing through my mind as the lady's voice broke through my thoughts and slightly stunned me.

"What the heck was THAT?" It's like this huge weight has just been lifted off me, all of me feels lighter. I can only tell how heavy I felt now it's gone." I nodded.

"Our systems understand so much through comparison so we drastically sense the difference in our aura when a heavy energy has been removed. It's like waking to a bright sunny spring morning after a long dark winter."

I kept the details minimal. No preconceptions in her were important to ensure the healing that would follow. Soon she departed, pale blue protection shielding her. Booked to return the following week.

Thankfully there was a good window of time to thoroughly electrically cleanse the whole centre. The purifying power of violet would have swept the residues up in its path, but the ceremony of chiming and incensing invited many elemental helpers and cleansing essences in. The building audibly sighed with the easement and stillness it created. Meanwhile my gut was telling me a whole new level of learning was afoot yet again.

Duly, the next day, I received a call from a very trusted healer friend. A thoroughly professional Reiki teacher too. It had been apparent from the moment I met her that her healing experience did not just span years, but many lifetimes. Together we cycled around in our student teacher roles, glad of each other's approach and the wisdoms we could share to assist each other. Her particularly acute intuition always brought me exactly the guidance I needed at the time.

Indeed, this very lady had lent me the very book I had drawn the needed insight from the previous day. My antennae all stood to attention. The timing of this contact was beeping an alert, and I was holding my breath in anticipation of what she was about to relay.

"I need to tell you this message that came through for you in a dream last night," she began. Now, it's very visual to be given a 'heads up' through a prophetic dream. But, my own experience of these had shown me that by majority they occurred with me, or for me as a precursor warning or signal to 'be ready'. And some had been a total download into my semi- conscious mind of the pathways and best choices to make within the most difficult times that were imminent.

Akin to pre-living the experience, time travelling ahead of this planetary 'reality', so all the systems are coded in full with the steps to tread on the journey ahead, in the very safest way possible. Like there is a speciality team of Sherpa guides within and with you, who know your unique makeup, character and qualities and from this can map a route of navigation that is most true to you. With the least pitfalls and the greatest degree of safety and efficacy. Where, oh where were they taking me now?!

She continued, "In the dream I was taken into a bookshop, led to a shelf and told, 'The next book that falls into your lap will hold the title that is the guidance you seek at this time'.

"A book duly materialized, I read the title, thanked them and put it back. Then they said this next book is for

Sue. And duly another book fell into my hands. The title, Sue, was 'The Exorcist'. I thought it wise to let you know.

"Now, do you thank friends that bring you news that feels as welcome as pork chops at a Jewish barbeque?" I was struggling to summon a coherent response. But, as always, the wisdom of her years held exactly the counsel they had ensured the message would travel with. "Remember in terms of our work, we are ever exorcist on that which needs to be transmuted and transformed. I think however the Universe has got some bigger plans ahead and that will have always been intended when the time is right. So trust, Sue, trust, listen acutely and they will guide."

She was right. No room for fanciful imaginings or preoccupations. Stay present and accept the present gifted! So I duly thanked her, assuring her that the timing was, yet again spot on. How wonderful the network they ever strengthened of this community of minds and hearts. A few days later, whilst out shopping, they decided to show me how it's done!

I found my feet marching me through the doors of a huge bookshop, three floors high! Up the stairs my feet went to the first floor. By then I knew to surrender to the 'fun', the guidance and my own systems were around. Without hesitation my legs strode over to a bookshelf and they said, 'Go on, just pick the book that's calling to you!'

I reached out, pulled a book and through one eye looked at the title.

'Memoirs of an Exorcist' lay in my hands! "Ah fuck off!" I said mentally, for the second time that week! I could hear their laughter as I paid for it. And what amazing help it proved to be. I still wonder how many hundred thousand books were in that massive bookshop and, of those, how many could possibly have Exorcist in the title!? So, head up, heart centred and feet planted, I squared up to the journey awaiting me. So far I had not fallen over, handed in my notice, or run off screaming... so far...so good!

Part 2

My feet felt like tree roots anchored far down into the earth's core. Rock solid stability. Needed like the resilient magnitude of an ancient mountain endurance. For the lady had returned, now so visibly amidst nervous exhaustion the couch shook as she lay there. "I felt much better, Sue, for a couple of days and then it all just hit me again. It's like being suffocated. I meditate and try to find calm but the walls close in on me. I feel trapped. Please make it stop."

The relief of shedding those layers had not even lasted a week. Tough, grimy work for such small reprieve. My concern was the toll it was taking on her. But layers had to be worked through at the pace both, the healing and the recipient's, systems set. And something strongly was confirming that all were gathering fast to nail it this time completely. For nothing had ever nailed my feet so firmly to the ground before.

As the earthing energy ran through me, rivers of it poured into her. Little by little the trembling eased to a quiver and peace descended. The stillness and light of a blanket of snow. However, the crescendo of forces present were deafening me. My body was alight. Mind as clear as a crystal wand. Words soothed, eyes scanned. Hands selected coloured silks. Something else took charge of every precise movement, pace and tone. I observed as its experience sensed, laid on silks and absorbed the many signals and signs.

"Take some deep breaths now. Say what you see when I ask you. Describe what you are led to only when I say. Trust the healing. Believe in the intelligence of your body." I held her hand tightly. Whatever lay ahead we could do this I knew.

Straight into travelling along the lines of connections. Everything is alert, acute to every visual picture, sound and smell. I almost cried when we arrived at the point. At the place where the extreme fears and panic originated.

"Trapped"- Oh yes. "Walls closing in on me." Dear Lord this was dreadful. A horrendous way to die. A terrible cruel act to perpetrate on another.

The darkness was suffocating. Abject loneliness, hunger and desolation wracked every sinew in me. She had been walled in. Put in a space and a wall built around her, stone by stone. It was so clear. Teeth clenched hard. I shook myself out of the feelings in me it was causing.

Absolutely no space for those. The tree roots beneath my feet shot deeper and wider. Pull yourself together right now! A command, not a request. My spine straightened. The focus of my eyes toughened to flint-like penetration. The 'I' that I knew was not looking through them. That gritty core in my stomach grew to granite. "Talk to her now," they bid. "We are going to remove what holds her there, and take down that wall together."

"What do you see?" I asked. "What are you recalling?" Tears rolled down her cheeks, shaking overtook her again. "A really horrible memory, a visual picture I was taken to when I did a Journey Healing Process." "The Third One?" I asked. "Yes, how do you know?" "Usually is," I replied, "Go on." "I truly thought it was gone, was remedied. I forgave the perpetrator to set myself free."

In a Journey Process you travel to a place in your body your intelligence takes you to. That point will be where a cellular memory lies that is key to healing the physical ailment or issue you are seeking to resolve. The process is very powerful and effective. That memory will reveal root causes, times, people, places involved in the causation of the 'problems' being worked on. On from this is a special ceremony, designed to bring resolve and settlement. I did not know the client had experienced Journey work. Fortunately I too had and knew how very accurate and powerful it is. Much work was already in place. But the emotional scars were too engraved for forgiveness alone to remedy them.

And I knew too how strongly parts of the body, through the cellular memories, are held in the past, reliving the trauma. A constant echo memory, emitting distress calls, that lie at the root of behaviours, addictions, phobias and physical and mental disorders and more. "Tell me," I encouraged. "I was taken to this place in my body each time I went for Journey work. It helped to ease anxiety and panic attacks a lot. Then I seemed to go very deep, like I was boring into the core of the symptoms and it made me really scared. Being near this cellular memory was so dark and miserable, and frightening. But the practitioner was really skilled and she asked me to describe what I was seeing and feeling. So, I managed to and I was so relieved as not only could she see it too, she also had the meaning and she had seen all that had happened."

Urging her to not take herself too deeply into that past process, she continued to describe what the practitioner had seen. "I had been left to die walled up." Tears streamed. Violent shaking overtook her. I gripped her hand tighter. "Stay here and now with me." Quiet, firm, reassuring, "I see that too. I know this to be true too. Now what else did she see?" The lady breathed deeply. Her bravery was stunning. "It's lifetimes ago. A deep trauma, soul print carried over. I had been a Nun," she said, "many times. But in this incarnation I developed a really close friendship with another Nun. We truly and purely bonded like actual sisters. Our love for each other was so incredibly rich. But, the Nun in charge was very jealous of us and saw it as sinful. So she separated us. Told us not to speak or see each other. But I sneaked out to see her, I missed my dear 'sister' so much. And that's when she caught me. And walled me up. Left me to die. To punish me and my dear sister too in the cruellest way possible."

Well now I knew where that dark entity originated from! Such wickedness. Was she seeking resolve, release too? My mind was instantly pulled away from that question. Not my concern. Focus, focus. Resolve this trauma now.

Thanking her, and the practitioner, for brave work and insight already done, I confirmed that this all made complete sense to what I had been shown and experienced. "But how will I escape this?" she cried. Reassuring her that now we had a clearer understanding, we were already 50% of the way to the solution. I took her hand and began to tap through the meridian EFT points.

"Close your eyes. Allow your body to guide. I am going to follow its lead to let go of all the emotions that hold you in that space. You are going to break out and your inner lives will show the way. They are ready now to set themselves free."

Never had I tried to work on a past life trauma so severe in this way. But all I could see were green lights. The way was clear, the truth was spoken and the doorways of the soul were wide open, calling. And no way was this vile blemish upon it from another's actions going to haunt her life any longer. As I tapped, the tuning into and with the lives within were ever more far reaching. Our conversation flowed. The plethora of those inner lives have so many varying characteristics. Born not only of the specific system and element they are a part of, but also the persona of the person themselves. A magical elemental blend of intelligences. And, in this case, everyone was wielding a tiny sledgehammer metaphorically. Oh yes, they were going to break free. Heal this hurt they felt, for all lived alongside and every cell knows of each other's joys, trauma and pain.

Thus, with expert guidance, path finding and a chorus of instructions, we worked on and on. Layer after layer. After over an hour had passed, of grim, shocking and horribly challenging work within that dark walled up cell, we had cleansed, transformed and erased each emotion, every cut and scar of trauma and shock. Together we had finally pulled that dear life to her feet and led her to the gap in the wall. Created by those sledgehammers and visual work to break through stone by stone, each and every harm we eradicated. She scrambled up and out and through, falling to the ground beyond with a loud cry of release. 'I' followed her desperate for air

To feel the grass. Breathe in the scent of flowers and trees. Hear the welcome buzz of insects and calls of birds again! Success! This time she was truly free.

An audible cry of relief rang out from the couch confirming the journey had been travelled. We tapped round the EFT points together affirming aloud, "I am now set free from all that held me there," over and over. Relief flooded her features.

A brand new ray of calm washed over and through her. The shaking abated. That eternal whirring of the adrenal glands, locked in fight or flight, pumping out adrenaline, ever fleeing, but never escaping, began to cease, to calm. The healing worked on, recalibrating kidneys, adrenals, organs and systems. Over time the blood system would find a new wonderful balance as the adrenaline that had constantly been pumped into it levelled off to normality at last. Nerve endings would no longer be constantly hyper actively alert. The body would no longer need to create the attacks of panic that were needed to exhaust each system's overload to avoid a heart attack or stroke. It had finally escaped the danger, the unspeakably awful fears and torture at last.

I tapped on. Thanking the inner lives' vast intelligence network, mine included. Whoops of joy, happy elemental lightness rang out. At last, the cellular sisters and brothers that had been locked in such distress and poor well-being were clear and free to begin their lives anew. So many revelations about the interconnectedness of it all. I had been witness to, party to, a miracle of far greater insight and understanding than ever before. It was a rare treasure to embed. And never had I seen such pure innocence and serene beauty shine through this lady's features. It had been like placing a snuffer over a candle flame, but now an ethereal glow was radiating, no longer stifled, snuffed out, the flame alive and free again.

Although everything seemed to be in order and two hours had passed by, I knew I was being called to go deep into the visual space and check everything was complete. The pictures would show me how the resolve was working to fresh beginnings and if there was any 'mopping up' to do! She was tired now, but settled down blissfully and I grounded and returned to the visual journey.

Like gently unfurling butterfly wings, freedom stretched out before me. Two soul sisters meeting in warm embrace at last. Rejoicing in their unified love, liberated and now carefree. Yes, those soul prints were healed. The Akashic records would celebrate a lift in their energy field, for one such healing works on behalf of the many. A goal scored for light and truth! I scanned the aura, the chakras, and the inner systems. Much rejigging and sorting going on! They know their work. "All in hand," they chorused, "We've got this now."

My mind felt the permission to project the question, "Anything else to do? To attend to?"

'Observe the violet ray do its work' came back. To experience its full power was astonishing. Indomitable. Decided. The last rites of purification and transmutation. Energy cannot be destroyed. It can only be changed. And violet is the Master of Finality and Decision to where, and for what that residual force will now serve as food. No longer to feed off other life parasitically, but instead be food for what can use it to serve the best purpose possible.

Organic life is a massive processing plant that cycles through reuse and clean-up to fresh issues constantly. But when the violet ray is called for, banishment to other realms is clear to witness. For there is no sustenance in that force even fit to feed a reptile. It is truly waste and earth has no use for it at all. The wonders of detoxification and purification within nature, within our body, within the Universe are extraordinary systems to observe and reflect on. Yes, indeed, 'Cleanliness is next to Godliness' and indigo and violet are gateways and gatekeepers that keep the Universe clean.

Together, the client and I gave our heartfelt thanks to everything. And we hugged for some time. "You are one of the kindest, gentlest and bravest souls I know," I told her. "Be proud of who and what you are and go forward now and live and enjoy. But also live for Yourself and Your own happiness first too." Once she had departed, and much cleaning had been achieved, I sat for some time reflecting on the deeper sense of knowing and understanding the healing had opened the door to. The vast world of sensory connections between the cells. That sense of true community and family and team work. The magnitude of experiences held in each tiny cell. And the way the well-being of the whole is affected by every single part of itself.

Each healing now lay in front of me like jigsaw puzzles, where the promise of missing pieces could be found and correctly placed. So the prospect of the holistic picture of life could be brought into focus and shine like a glossy polaroid. This was what exorcism of darker forces and unthinkable traumas could bring. Yes, dirty, harrowing and tough it was, but who had said the only place success comes before work is in the dictionary?

The ring of my phone broke through the reflections. An excited voice, clear and strong. "Sue, I have never ever felt like this before. My whole life I have been weighed down and dogged by background fear. Always feeling trapped and anxious and hopeless to it. The change is breathtaking. I feel so alive and free. It's gone, all gone and I can't begin to express how grateful I am." Reminding her that the flow of gratitude had many roads to travel but I was filled with gladness to hear her joy, I returned to my reflections.

Eventually, clear and centred, I declared out loud, "Where do I sign? Because I will never run away. Whatever your bid and call I am here as a willing volunteer and recruit."

Donning my coat, (Lord did I need a shower!) their reply drifted into my ear like a cheeky whisper. "You signed up eons ago. The ink is well and truly dry on that contract my friend." Winking my right eye to them I drove home to the welcoming arms of the water elementals blissfully cleansing every smudge of darkness away. Piped hot water into our homes. What a grace to behold each day!

Chapter 13

Lessons from Darkness and light

Past Life Influences and Ancient Curses

Past Life influences and Ancient Curses

It was a welcome day off that dawned with brilliant sunlight. As its warmth seeped into the land, hazy shimmers of humidity danced in the air currents, atmospheres of the theatre of the elementals at play. Visually captivating, a dance of celebration of the heat and light. Below, the ground shed the frigid grip of cold and damp. Each cell of its being expanding, stretching like a lazy cat draped in front of the fire. In winter it is as if the Earth contracts, takes a long breath in. All life receives that signal and follows, disappearing into a variety of strata of hibernation.

Some simply sleep the season away. For them winter will ever be a dream state, until the arrival of spring entices them from their slumbers. The physical pangs of hunger, an innate compulsion to breed, to ensure continuance, propels them to emerge. Others migrate, for their life cycle is intrinsically interwoven with the mysteries of harmony and finite balance of nature herself. The power of the seasons. An eternal Passion Play with the cast of spirits of the elements ever influencing.

As buds appear, and light shrinks the hours darkness has stolen, the days expand again. All life unfurls anew. We shed our layers of heavy blankets and mummified hold of thick coats, woollens and hats. In sync with nature we gladly shake off the tight restrictive contraction, unfurling and blooming besides the buds' release. The continual master, the patterns and pathways of the sun, its influence compelling all life, akin to the compass needle incapable of resisting magnetic north.

Yes, a perfect day off for the planned walk with a friend! But, the elementals had not awoken me with their best dance moves to woo me on a day off! A full and welcome day with nature was, for them, an opportunity not to be missed. For the elements never down tools and disappear into 24 hours of R and R, so there is no 'day off' in their vocabulary!

After many hours of glorious remote hills, we decided to explore a village nearby. Drawn by the Church spire, we studied it on approach, and slipped quietly through the churchyard gate. The original stone building was ancient, but someone of Victorian landed gentry had been 'honoured' with a large octagonal extension added to the side. It was a carbuncle of quite epic proportions, and sat uneasily next to the much subtler vibrations of what still resonated within its origins of a once tiny chapel.

The stone interior exuded a chill that starkly contrasted the warmth outside. No stranger to sensing ley lines, our feet felt locked onto the power line that ran straight up the middle of the aisle. But neither of us headed for the altar. Instead our complete focus was magnetized by what once was purely a small rudimentary place of worship, which lay to the right of the main body of the church. Something was calling us. Energy climbed to a clear buzzing whistle, activating the crown chakra and causing the Third eye to pulse. Not something, someone. A male energy. And a highly connected and developed one too. What could he need? He knew, no way could I resist.

As we entered the walls seemed to be shimmering with fine, high vibrations. My attention was on the old stained glass window. Quite extraordinary in its muted colours of pale greens and browns. Perhaps faded with age, but it had never been garish. It seemed incredibly important to note what it depicted, so on tip toes I studied the details. Simple bundles of threshed wheat and loaves of bread. As I committed it visually to mind the energy shifted and I wobbled off balance. What was the significance here of bread, symbol of physical sustenance for life? The presence was making its importance clear. And I was realizing all had been waiting, anticipating our arrival. As always my plans really were another architect's 'blueprints'.

As I turned I realized my companion had been standing transfixed by a very ancient crypt. The stonework, although ornate, was simple. Crafted to afford, through beautifully shaped apertures, a view of the slab over a stone grave far below. Atop, the huge slab was worn smooth by the many thousands of hands that had touched it. All around this clearly sacred altar crypt lay pieces of paper and flowers and petals long since dried. Faded words, still visible on some yellowed parchment. Others starkly contrasting, bright white with ink clear against the background. She was engrossed in the process of reading. Each was carefully replaced before another was selected. Her face was wet with tears.

As I began to read the messages and prayers my eyes brimmed too and spilled with the weight of emotions. This had become a shrine. Clearly the ancient grave below held the remains of a very Holy Wise Man and healer. His legend had long endured and generation after generation had knelt to feel his blessing, words of counsel and pray to receive his healing powers. From the spidery letters of an aging hand asking that one long loved be received into the arms of God, to the tiny hands new to grasping a pen who implored, "Please make Grandma better", an ocean of emotions lay in every swirl and letter. And for certain the recipient of all these pleas was standing right next to me. What could such an evolved life long gone from earth's plane be reaching out to us for?

Held, united in silent prayer, eventually my friend broke the spell, "What is here with us? For something is impressing its need upon us!" I hesitated. She was not new to quite radical deeper experiences, but from the road travelled of late I had a feeling this could be another rough single track journey along a cliff edge.

However, I did not own the copyrights on the life scripts they were writing for me. If something had sprung this on us today then it clearly intended us to take this trip together. "The life who is urgent appears to be whoever this very revered saintly man whose resting place lies below this shrine was. There was a sudden energy shift at the window. Noting the bread, sustenance is relevant to his story. But, I feel this is like the wise hermit in Samos. It's a call for something he needs and this place, this land here. So, there is healing to do. We have to just find out what."

She was nodding enthusiastically so I suggested we go outside and see where we were led to next. Straight through the entrance, into the ancient church yard, both of us by passing the two tall Celtic crosses that dominated. Instead, a grave across from them drew us to it. The inscription told of a very dearly adored long serving reverend of the church hundreds of years prior. He too was drawing us like a magnet. Exuding a compelling passion for this parish.

Powerfully adding his voice to his fellow Holy Men's call.

Suddenly a strong aroma surrounded us. The unmistakable scent of sweet ripe fruit. It was akin to standing at a greengrocer's market stall enjoying the mixed aromas of apples, plums, bananas, cherries and more. We stared around us in surprise. Not a fruit tree or bush in sight. "Oh my word!" she declared. "The scent of fruit by a grave. That's incredible!" I was poised.

Clearly she had some intelligence about this! I only heard this understanding a week ago. "If a soul has built its development beyond planetary, meaning it has birthed aspects of itself in higher dimensions and no longer HAS to reincarnate here to learn and develop further - there are certain aromas that signify this. The scent of flowers is saintly and of the highest possible to achieve here. The next level is the fragrance of fruit. This reverend too achieved an extraordinary level of compassion and high embodiment as a human life here. This church and land has been graced by at least two very high spiritual presences."

We felt no compulsion to move away from this gentle compassionate energy. Nor the wonderful sweet perfume saturating the air all around us. It was as if our saintly guide desired not only energy be evoked, re-awoken, but also willed this resting place too, to be known as a shrine. A wash of humility coursed through. He too was emitting waves of reverence for this life. Almost as if he felt it even greater, purer than his own. Something was deeply troubling this dear wise presence. A call that had long cried from within echoed through me.

He had connected us into the frequency and point of this disruption on his energy field and life path. There was a deep disturbance and it lay somewhere between him and this place, this land. And now we had the protection of a most developed spirit with us too. Thus, armed with another highly evolved Holy Essence and a mindful wondering of how many of my friends would have had that particular piece of the puzzle. We stood in unison and turned left out of the churchyard gate. Not a falter of hesitation, for now the land was calling too.

Determined strides towards the river straight ahead. Meandering along its direction of flow to the right in the distance, a pathway snaked, disappearing from sight into thick wooded cover.

Evocative of the call of the land in Samos the currents of force carried us. Past a huge baptismal pool. Onward. Driven. Our feet pounding. Ahead my companion continued towards the river, to the huge stone bridge spanning it. An uneasiness surged. My feet stalled, incredulous at the appearance before me. Never before had I met such an earth elemental. His form and demeanour were stocky, stout and extremely gruff. "NO, you do not cross the bridge," he transmitted angrily. As the words reverberated through me like a bellow he raised his right arm and pointed a stubby finger towards the woodland path. Casting a derisory glance that told me he thought I was a rather ugly being to his eyes, which I received with a sense of shame, he then disappeared as fast as he had manifested. Thoroughly chastised, I gathered enough presence of mind to both apologize for my rudeness and thank him for the directions, before quickly taking the route.

As I vowed to reconsider all the tales of Trolls guarding bridges, as for sure I had just met one, I wondered if the paying of a 'toll' had derived from those times when humans and elementals shared awareness and their lives harmoniously? For such an earth elemental would be incredibly industrious. Intrinsically a part of the very fabric and maintenance of the land he was endemic to, and the spiritual life force of. And the safety and integrity of a structure such as a bridge is vital. Just like the offerings of petals and flower garlands beside wells, thanking the water elementals for their life and crop preserving grace and bounty, I realized humans then too had made a return for the stability of ground and rocks and safe passage thus over the water. As insight trickled through, borne from the fortune of being within their unique energy field, I could sense the Troll's childlike acceptance. It was a grumpy note of forgiveness, but as humans go, at least I'd seen, heard and listened and redeemed myself a bit!

Catching up with my friend, who I thought had stopped to rest, as she had veered onto the pathway too at quite a pace when the elemental appeared. However, not one word did she utter about the troll, instead her gaze was fixed on the dark shadows inches from her feet. It was as though a foreboding tunnel lay ahead. Waiting, hungry, to swallow us up. "Listen," she implored, "It's just eerily silent. Not a bird chirping. Nor an animal rustling. Yet soon it will be dusk." She was right. Silence. Total absence of life.

The sunlight had dimmed. Dark clouds hung over the woods. Its canopy reached up, twisted, distorted, like skeletal fingers and limbs, suspended helplessly, arthritic and deformed. Deep breaths, and together we inched forward into the gloom. The creeping sense of entering a catacomb enveloped us. The entire woodlands' souls laid bare before us. Energetically dead. Devoid of any presence of life within flora and fauna alike. Urgent whispers, crying for senses to see its misery. The purgatory it was held in. The true reality of its being.

Slowly, horribly spell bound, we moved deeper in. All around us twisted, knotted, entwined trunks and branches, which seemed to have sought solace by binding themselves to each other. No sight of bird life. No rustling leaves announcing life scurrying in the ground. No squirrels leaping and playing. Nothing. It was a petrified forest, long removed from its vitality. Locked in this ever-foreboding atmosphere of decay.

"What has happened to you?" I asked aloud. Focus intensified. My concern for the woods, for the Holy man's plight, now greater than that for my friend. Waves of urgency. We moved on farther, continuing to a point where the entrance to a cave opened in the rock face to the right of the path. A clear spring pool lay below the gaping chill of its entrance. The Saint had drunk from this source. Drawn water daily and lived in this forest. His desire surged to thank its life source. To mark this place with his gratitude. Moments passed. The bidding came to retrace some steps.

Just ahead of me my friend's feet skidded to a stop. Her eagerness to be released from the death grip of the place was clear, but now she was staring to the left of her, bemused. "Did you see these steps when we came through here?" she called. I indeed had not. They were old, worn and led up a steep bankside. We could glimpse a sheer rock side edge above. My feet were climbing before the brain could question. And the higher I climbed the more certainty nudged that the destination lay just ahead, waiting.

The last step. A large rocky plateau. And in front of a now enclosed cave mouth I knew to have been the Saint's Hermitage, stood a very heavy, rough ancient stone table and rudimentary bench. Beside it, the presence of an old man. Exuding sadness, mirroring the despair of the woodland, an aura of misery imprisoning him. He beckoned me to sit. To place my hands upon the stone. The ache in my gut was unbearable. I maneuvered uncomfortably around the huge stone table top and sat down on the cold, damp bench.

"This man is locked in desperate misery," I whispered. "His guilt is like a knife in my guts." She stood, pained, tearful. "I feel it too. It's like he and the woods are held in one huge sadness together." I stared hard at her. "Trust me. And stay totally still."

My hands rose from my abdomen and placed themselves flat upon the stone surface. His presence moved into me and I heard her gasp in fear. All of me, all of him and all of the woods became one. A rush of impressions. His crying voice echoed throughout my body. "We hear your confession. We hear you. All knows. All receives. All forgives." I soothed. Tears flowed.

Relief and pain flooded from his being. From every tree and woodland life form. My body ached. Ravaged by age and pain. Bent and twisted with the gnarled state of ancient bones.

"No more guilt." Choruses of elemental spirits and essences barmed, the whispers falling loud on ears that had been locked in silence for so long. In our communion all now was clear. I understood. Our united sighs ricocheted down and up the timelines of energy, like a heartbeat, steadying, falling into a rhythmic even pulse.

"Now all will heal. Will renew and recover. The spell is broken. Your soul print here and the woods are released." My hands stayed on the table until the aching pains ebbed and died away. With each wave of relief his presence receded further until finally I became detached, my awareness singular once again. Within, all the cells seemed to be recalibrating, shifting, vibrating. Never before had I felt both nature and a presence overtake me so completely. The trust was all encompassing. Driven by the need. Safe within the integrity of all concerned. Glad to have been so accepted and allowed to serve the call. Eyes closed, I waited. My bones were slowly recovering from their arthritic state and the soreness in my abdomen was being deeply soothed by healing hands. Eventually I shifted position and peeled my hands from the table.

On opening my eyes, my friend's face swam into view.

"Are you ok?" she stammered. "Your hands went gnarled and old as soon as you touched the table. And then your whole body aged and bent. Was the Hermit the Saint from the church?

What happened when he lived here in these woods?"

I stretched carefully, sliding gingerly out from the chillingly cold slab. "He had cursed the woods. Ahead I will know why. That matters not at this moment in time. It was a very ancient curse. His remorse and guilt had held a part of him here. There had been no escape. For him, the elementals, nature and his soul print just locked in eternal mourning. He needed to feel their forgiveness. To join with them to hear his confession. Together they broke free and were released from its hold. He, the elementals and the healing brought us here to break the spell.

And he ensured we had the protection of a devout Holy Man alongside us all the way. We knew that church spire drew us in today! But that was a pretty full on initiation so I hope you're ok!"

As she nodded, relieved, the silver dance of dusk sprang into life. A single note of cheer from a bird's beak rang out and a chorus of calls and responses surged. "It is broken!" she exclaimed. Yes, before our eyes life blood seemed to be coursing through root systems, sap rising, nourishing, feeding and replenishing the dry twisted branches. And hot on the back of such massive regeneration, I knew exactly what would come next. "Come on," I called, hurrying in the direction of the car. "It is going to now rain like you have never seen before!"

Always after a huge healing the cleansing from the elements is astonishing. Big, fat, cold raindrops were falling before we reached the sanctuary of the car. But we had barely started the engine before thunder began to crash and lightning lit up the skies. It was a dramatic 45-minute drive home. A most fitting encore to complete all my friend had witnessed! And a few days later, eager to research, I discovered even more than I had believed possible to weave the threads together with awe and wonder in every stitch!

The shrine crypt in the church lay above the grave of an early 8th Century Hermit called Saint Bertram or Bertelin. Over his resting place in medieval times the altar had been built. His wisdom and healing powers had been greatly revered and carried throughout the ages. People from all corners of the earth travelled to his altar shrine. Two holy wells, where baptisms and healings were performed still stand - one by the large baptismal pool next to the church, and the other by the cave the Saint had lived in. The bridge the 'Troll' guarded is known as St Bertram's Bridge. And yes, the depiction of bread and wheat in the stained glass window that caused such a 'shock' is very poignant to the dear Saint and Hermit's story. For the most stark point in his life, that caused his solitary long existence in the cave began at what would have been his happiest young days when the promise of life stretched ahead of him.

The account of his life records that he was a Mercian Prince who travelled to Ireland to marry the love of his life. Later, together, they travelled to England. By then his wife was heavily pregnant and she gave birth safely in those woods. He left them to go in search of food and on his return found the wolves had killed his beloved wife and newborn baby. It was from that point he became a Hermit, living in the cave and became sought after by many for his wisdom and healing powers. Over twelve hundred years later his legacy endures.

As I read of his life, St Bertram entrusted me with his personal account…

"But from that dreadful day, as much as healing aided others, my own grief endured, and alone, my suffering overcame me. I cursed the woods. Locked it into my sorrow, pain and mourning, believing it should share the hurt. And we know the truth of the Healer is 'If you can heal, so too can you harm'. I and the woods became so deeply entrenched in that pain and sorrow until there was no way for me to lift the curse, for now I was too a part of that curse. We became one. Eternally condemned to our misery. Unable to set each other free. For the woods' very soul and spirit beings felt as guilty as I. And then you came. Two lives who could hear me, see the truth in our souls and break the spell. Set us free at last."

I was deeply moved by the trust and faith from all. For some time after I sent distance healing to the woods to power and support their regeneration. And sometime later the river called to me to take a colour and crystal water remedy according to its requests. The day I took it, all bade me to cross the bridge. To drip the healing elixir into the body of its energy flow. To travel and fill the land with the newfound joy. It was like a baptism heralding new starts, new beginnings for every dear elemental being.

That day I returned to the window. The bread and wheat in their muted greens and browns taking me to the heart of the truth of the Hermit Saint's pain. For its depiction represented this Prince as a Holy Man. Held the key to both, his high acclaim and revered fame, but also his pain. For it was said that the Devil tempted him to turn stones to bread. But being a righteous man with honour in his heart, he would not abuse the powers vested in Him in such a self- serving way. The Devil tempted him but he refused. His choice thus elevated the trust in his high development. Charged his life with powerful healing energies and foresight. Created the path of the Wise and Holy Man whose legacy endured, of great acts and deeds. However, privately, the pain within him never healed.

Years had passed before I sat to fully record this account for this book. As with every chapter, accuracy to, and for that which you have served and worked is vital. They choose the words to explain and bring in the understandings of the realms they inhabit. As I neared the end the Hermit blessed me with another secret of his soul he wished to now be understood. I hold great gratitude for His permission to pass this on:-

"The stone table I led you to was the most profound point of connection because my pain and torment began with the rocks, the stones. Yes, I could have called on those powers, my connection with the elements and elementals, to turn those rocks into bread. But as a Holy Man, a devout life, I decreed those as the Saviour's powers. Not for me to call upon and use for my will and need. So, I upheld my faith and in that moment I chose this path of Saintliness, of solitary piety, over a life with my dearest of loves. For, although their hunger was a great need, so too was my need and will to do right. And, in making that choice I left them to search for food. And on my return they were dead. Had become food for the animals in the woods. Never then could I leave that place again. And we, I and those dear woods slowly petrified and died inside together from guilt and shame. The curse I put upon it caused any chance for us to choose life ahead again to wither and die away too.

For my faith my wife and child died. If I had turned those rocks to bread I would not have gone to seek food. But I would have abused the power gracing me. And of all the elements I cursed Earth, the rocks and stones the most. The deepest connection to the sorrow, ache within and harm was through the rock. But then you came and the elements trust you. They trusted you to set them free."

How powerful our choices are. And how deeply interconnected as one we are with the entirety of this earth, all life forms and the Universe. I asked the Saint one question, "Would you make that same choice again?"

"Yes," he replied without hesitation. "And you, you do truly know why, don't you?"

A very deep ancient core in me knew. "Because we have already chosen integrity, truth and honour. And in so doing the rock will stay a rock. Just as the Gods decreed. It is not our place to change its destiny nor to alter ours. But to learn it is found through surrender and acceptance. And the hardest times in life's journey will often be where we make the greatest returns."

We bless the rocks together and part. The richest of experiences. With the wisest and Highest of Lives. Borne out from surrender. And the honour of Acceptance.

Chapter 14

The Lawless Land

Some years had now passed since the house cleanse that had instantly begun, on arrival, as a whole land mass clearing. Since then, being imbued into re-balance for land had stayed very clearly defined from the requests to settle homes or business premises.

And whilst always, attention to the ground a building sat upon was woven into every process, none had escalated to that scale since. However, even as I read through this email from a couple requesting help with 'unrest' they were experiencing in their home, a creeping sense of intrigue seeped through about it and just how far reaching these went.

So, calendar out, I sensed ahead for what felt right to proceed. The day lay a little over a month ahead. Pre-work was called for. Considerable time and focus had to be made to answer this call.

In making contact with them, I was left with relief at their openness and warmth, but also a sense of much greater mixed dynamics at play, reaching way beyond their 4 walls and boundary. Threads of connections were springing up, like a veritable minestrone soup of energies. It felt unlikely that I would just be able to pick the carrots and onions out and declare the soup was now a consommé so all clear!

This had a challenge written all over it and I was flying solo that day. Finding a date when Donna and I could dedicate a whole day together pushed the cleanse far beyond what all had already got planned.

Remote sensing quickly became remote viewing expeditions. The cottage had an awful lot of confusion, and it was ultra-keen to talk to me about them. The various extensions hovered faint and barely formed alongside the original very old building, mere appendages, add ons that it held no affinity for within its sense of self. As the reality of the structure pulled me back and back towards its 'youth', its raw and rudimentary beginnings imprinted pictures in my mind. I could see the big thick stone fireplace still standing in what had been a scullery type kitchen. The sheer volume of focus, process and importance that pivots around a hearth is huge. From dawn to the later hours of the night, tending to its 'needs' to provide warmth and the nourishment of cooked simple food creates a vortex of imprints. And, within that hundreds of lives huddled around it, sharing every human story imaginable. And some better left unimagined. And the older a place, the more potent and over printed that fireside will be. Indelibly etched as the heart of the very fabric and body of that place. So, removing a hearth, blocking up a chimney, taking away the physicality of that structure, will always hugely affect a building in the very soul of its being. However, this place was showing me it was still proudly intact. But, a deep disquiet and unease radiated from the heart of this home.

The print of a simple wooden narrow staircase lay to the side of the ancient stone hearth. It was clear the scullery had been extended to a kitchen over at least two phases and those stairs had been removed and relocated. Thus the structure was in great disquiet. Continually flashing me the same reality as if my being able to sense and visualize its truth would rebuild them and return the flow to its rightful place!

Eventually, the registrations began to gain a little order and dis-ease from the adjoining property impressed itself as the first issue. Not only did the structure itself feel most bizarre, the energy of the tenants renting it was beyond strange. They had caused unpleasantness from the outset, but the level of troublesome vibrations emanating from next door felt as if all behaved in ways that inferred neither laws or common decency applied to them. Similarly, the land seemed to be drenched with the same nature of energy. A large-scale map of the area was duly employed. Whatever was all this strangeness about?

Within the terrain lay rolling countryside and wooded areas. Small rows of houses amidst randomly dotted buildings sat within the setting which radiated sheer unrest and oddness. It was as if a perimeter fence marked this zone on the map defined as separate to the vast area it lay within. And its name glared at me from the centre. I searched for its meaning. 'Land under dispute' – ancient terminology. The plot was thickening. From way back in time a veritable can of worms lay wriggling! I very gingerly proceeded to lift the lid!

For a very long time that whole area had remained 'free land'. A veritable 'oasis' untouched and very soon untouchable by the very laws of the land. In many ways it had served a purpose. A kind of 'ghetto' where taxes were not paid and general trade and getting by depended on being artful, cunning, just generally operating outside of any laws anyway. It held a 'community' in the sense that all arose from a common denominator together. A veritable blend of colourful characters, outcastes, ladies of the night, petty criminals and thieves and those purely lost and wandering and living on their wits, who could not find some place within 'society'. Unwanted or unwilling to agree to a life of servitude and hard graft obeying a master. Why make the Lords of the Manor richer and pay a tithe with what you grew too when you could grow your own food for free here? Or buy from a butcher when you could poach in the woods? And ply your skills and goods, for those within 'accepted' society often had need to seek them and all possible to get within this 'lawless land'. So, over time the 'untouchables' became untouched in their exclusion zone. And for those on the outside, well it served a purpose of keeping the rough and tumble all together!

As I researched a good few hundred years' worth of frivolity, lawlessness, general debauchery and all manner of behaviours, lifestyles and characters impressed themselves upon me. For many a last chance saloon. For others just the opportunity they sought! And that sense of honour among thieves also rang like a bell. Its wild freedom from constraints compelled me.

Just beyond the perimeters evidence appeared of smiling raggedly dressed children as rudimentary schooling became available in later years. Overtones of religion also trying to impress itself upon the inhabitants. Whether through desire to gain some control or genuine will to respond to human need, that sense of a deeply embedded and entrenched way of life had driven prints into that area of land like heavy cart wheel tracks.

Clearly children born there would personify the lifestyle, through no other exampleship or ability to escape it, without some form of education and insight into other ways to live and be. I traced back over three hundred years of its very distinct history as an 'exclusion zone'. And of course written records first hand did not exist, so only the worst of its past could be found.

Within trials for theft and crime and frowned upon behaviour that found its way into print. Such an assorted bag of impressions I had never remotely viewed and sensed before. And the rebel in me felt delighted by it. Whilst another life in me was groaning, 'What the heck are they getting us mixed up in, this TIME?'

"One step at a time with clear intention." Gentle guidance ever present. However, I still felt like a traveller wandering into the desert armed with factor 6 sun cream. Well trained and boot camped to not play with fire and get my fingers burned, cautions ran through me as I assembled numerous crystals and items together as they bid. Staring at the seemingly random selection alongside the map I felt lost in the wondering of what pre-work they could possibly have planned? "Now I've got all the gear and absolutely no idea," I said aloud. Movements, shifts, the atmosphere jolted around me. That radiation of doubt was causing some serious prodding in my aura! Sometimes you need reminding to not offend your most trustworthy friends! Duly re-focused I centred and allowed myself to be led.

Many times before I had done distance work through maps but this time the process was very different. I had been guided to 4 particular crystals and objects and found one crystal and object each signified an element. These I was instructed to place on the 4 compass points surrounding the area. This was to be a 28-day process, encompassing one moon cycle, and each morning I was to focus on initial clearing of interruptive forces and presences through this layout. This would give a huge pre-connection with the endemic elementals, and it was clear how urgent they were to get to work. A human agency was all they needed and I had been captured already! So, I set this connective point of focus out under the cover of the decking area high above our home. Located amidst nature and the woods beyond it was the perfect place.

I quickly discovered this grid was very powerful indeed. Distance healing was vivid and images flashed at speed. In just 20 minutes each morning a huge swathe of work commenced and completed. They added a small bowl of fresh water to the centre of the grid and vapours of purifying energy emanated from it across the land.

Day 7, a Sunday dawned bright with a sense of change already palpable. 'The completion of the first cycle of 4,' I thought, just as my phone began to ring, displaying the number of the clients concerned. The lady's voice was full of excitement. "What have you been doing, Sue?" I gave a small summary of the process, keen to know what had occurred! "The neighbours are gone," she declared. "Without a word or prior indication they just packed up yesterday and left. All of their belongings are gone. And our home and we feel better already!"

Wow, those nature elementals sure know how to remove interruptive forces and presences fast! After sharing in her happiness I focused afresh. For holding that clearer space and attracting new occupants who would be considerably more convivial needed to be mindfully added to the daily projections. Nature cannot stand a void. I needed to ensure the vibration changed and attracted more agreeable tenants this next time around.

The agreed 28 days of potent distance work passed and the day dawned to go to the cottage. It was an hour's drive away but first I needed to walk into the woods beyond it as something was calling me, so I woke early, keen and ready. Driving past the cottage I parked by a footpath entering the woodlands. After a short walk, declaring my intentions and openness to its summons, I stood silently and waited. Like a magnet they pulled my focus to my feet where a twig from a fir tree lay. "Pick me up," it said. Obliging, I laid it across my right palm to receive its message. The intelligence and presence of the entire wood and lands all around resonated through the pine tree elemental. "You only need to carry with you one part of our being for us all to work with you. This is our gift together of communion. We are already joined and united.

Take us with you. This is your staff. We still have much work to do. And today will be joyful together."

What a gift! And such care. I stood rooted to the spot by the power of the intelligence and healing capacity within the organic worlds. My only prior reference for a staff were the words from the Bible, 'My rod and my staff shall comfort and protect me!' Which had led me to the understanding that within that very wood that formed the staff its nature elementals chose to travel consciously with you inside the fabric of its being. To guide and protect and call on others on your travels so you are secure and led specifically by those endemic to each particular land and frequency thereof. They had literally gifted me a Sat Nav! A personal guide with direct communication to air traffic control and ground staff!

Exclaiming lots of gratitude, I duly arrived at the cottage grasping my fir twig staff tighter than a hungry kid with a jammy dodger! Whatever lay ahead, the whole consciousness of this land was working with me. No way were they letting me fly solo!

After an equally warm welcome at the house I set to work. Various extensions and alterations did indeed feel like artificial limbs. Neither nerve or blood system of the original body of the structure felt physically or energetically joined. The main room's thick ancient stone walls held the echoes of strata of evolvements. Like layers of sediment each sitting uneasily above the other with the 'top tier' feeling like a half-devoured cake as part of the original structure now lay beyond a later constructed wall as a part of the next-door dwelling. It sat dishevelled in its sense of self amidst the carving up and many alterations suffered. And the line of lives it had given shelter and safety to stretched hundreds of years back. For sure the earliest of those being of the 4-legged variety. And in a far corner the offending staircase sat. Such an anachronism it barely felt either floor accepted it, so it appeared as if it hovered remote and unattached. Just a narrow simple construction but as welcome in that room as wasps at a picnic. My, a UFO parked in Tesco car park would have looked less out of place!

As I had passed through the kitchen the now familiar sight of the original stairs had impressed itself upon me even stronger. Leading me back to the time it had been little more than a rudimentary ladder construction leading up from the combined tiny scullery and living place by the fire. Above I could already 'see' the original sleeping platform where the heat of the stone chimneystack would have lent warmth to the sleeping forms amidst the stored hay and straw. I had entered via the kitchen and immediately became confused as it was not the doorway I had been 'entering' through. That lay to the left and now also blocked up. The home owners confirmed that, and the stairs they had changed which had enabled a further bedroom and bathroom and larger kitchen.

Three phases of extending and alterations had occurred in their hands, none of which the house either recognised or embraced as a part of itself.

Upstairs the disparity between original and new continued. With some trepidation I entered the bedroom from the landing now lacking its well-trodden stairwell. A lingering heavy sense stirred unease immediately. Memories locked in the thick stone walls wailing for release. Palpable unpleasant vibrations pulsing from the cottages' very cells, emitting from the fireplace's chimney stack. Tendrils of pain from under the windows. Wisps of sadness, vapours of intense fear, swirling and licking their way out from the cracks and crevices puttering like smoke from dry kindling sticks up through the vacuous sooty reaches of the ancient chimney. I pulled my senses away. Snapped out of the connection.

Some dark secrets from long ago. Hidden in the depths of the layers of the sediments of time. It seemed as if the weight of their very darkness had caused them to sink deeper into the layers. As if the dwelling itself wanted to push them into ground further and further away from its own being. It wanted them gone, cleaned, purified. To be rid of them finally. But I was sure there was much to do first to work to that layer's release. And today was not the time for that 'battle' to be fought. The shields had gone up. All that awaited to work had no intention of purging that dark zone today. Closing the bedroom door firmly, I grasped my staff.

Time to go outside for the garden in its elevated position was perfect to view the entire house from and cast into the flow of guidance.

Thirty minutes later, as the blue smoke filled and puttered to every corner and the familiar purification ensued, my mind was continually being pulled from focus to the staff alive in my hand and an ever-widening span of the land all around. The mental filaments stretched on, expanding so far and wide, way beyond the range and span of visual and sensory perception I had ever experienced before. Quivers of delight. Old friends in new acquaintances, long desired. A suspended sense of savouring the moment, like parted lovers at last captured in the embrace of reunion.

Trills of joy, calls of elation, ringing out from the vast expanse of open countryside and woodlands beyond and all around. My mentality held the consciousness of vast miles in every direction and thus, within and of that, a platoon of elementals more varied in kind and number than my systems had reference for, or capacity to compute.

In my hand lay the fir twig staff, but no sense of separation, of its being distinct from mine, now existed. For the atoms of our defined physicalities had melted into one. Blended in a rush of love, belonging and sheer elation of reconnection. I was in and of everything, just as it too was in and of me…. Swaying with each blade of grass dancing to the tunes of the wind… steadfast, strong in rocks and boulders enraptured by the permanence of earth's story…circling heady heights of lofty trees on birds' wings… no me, no them… only us, the pure unifying bliss of us united as ONE.

Captured now in that timeless truth our cellular whole vibrated in the wondrous reality of simply being whole again. Sparklers flared, fireworks crackled, the atmosphere alight with the merged vibrations of all nature and human essence rekindling a sacred relationship once so natural and yet now so rare. The Nirvana of arriving home to every loved soul in every lifetime sitting around the table together laughing, making merry. And seeing alongside and with them the essences and elemental energies combining and pulsing in their interplay. And then realizing there is a place set for you. The chair is pulled out, waiting. You have always been a part of this. Always been at home. You just have not joined the party before. Never quite taken your seat at the table of life here. But now at last, you have been wooed by the warm embrace of reunion and communion. Ever now to be held in the sweet release of surrender to its captivating spell.

And then, amidst the celebrations, words began to fill my head. Gentle but firm, they subtly opened my mind further to the part they required me to play. Through the unique make-up of the human design, they could restore and heal together. Most of all the way was forged for them to come together. So within the unified limitless consciousness it was now imperative to hold and maintain, all began to arrive and work together in a most extraordinary way. The old dwelling vibrated with the energies of hundreds of elementals, the very essences of the stones, wood, slate, every single fibre of its whole. And the strong, solid original oak beam held the most powerful presence of all.

It is not surprising that the 'Head house elemental' (or Head House keeper!) is often to be found in the main support of the building itself. And just as that physical presence is so crucial to the well-being and integrity of the whole structure, so too is the Elemental of the very beam itself.

Every building has tens of hundreds of elementals all working to maintain it. Within that is a leadership structure. And in this cottage all revered the Oak Beam Elemental not only for its strength and adhesion to maintaining, upholding the physical structure, but also for the great wisdoms held within every knot and ring. Knowings, so vast, of lived experience with the land itself. Intimately held connections to every tree and life form for miles around still standing since its own time as a huge oak amidst the forest had been cut short and changed by human hands. In reverence of the ancient oak, every elemental bowed. For miles around a silence fell as all connected with the wisest elder of that land. In the presence of greatness I aligned my whole with its power.

The collective consciousness of the Dryads began to form, through my mind's eye, the medium through which all would meet and work. I was about to see just how many connections they had strengthened and created during those 28 days of process!

I 'watched' from the peaceful space in the garden as a form akin to a giant energetic totem pole began to emerge. Totem poles were created as receivers and transmitters, to radiate and be receptive to specific signals and messages which were true to the land and the peoples upon it.

Neither the woods chosen for its form or the symbolic carvings and art upon it were arbitrary. All completely chosen to power the holding, integrity and purposes chosen as the tenets of that community. A radiant beacon through which the nature elementals of the land can work and communicate together through and thus enhance the telepathic conversations across the miles between tribes. Who could also place their hands upon specific trees and send messages to each other through the sacred pathways of the interconnecting underworld of the root systems between the family of trees. A natural network. The original world wide web.

When human systems atrophied, the senses dulled and disconnected by forced clearances and displacement to large towns or cities, telepathy withered, and ancient skills were lost.

Either the sheer need to survive through their lands being stolen and decimated caused the natural human sensitivity to ebb away. Or the search for money and cultural lures superimposed themselves over the true purposes and reasons for life and those natural talents waned, unnecessary within that different artificial ecology. Where trees and totems become telegraph poles, adorned with wires, a crude replacement to the natural human ability. Telephones replacing what the design can actually do for itself!

But the trees were about to show me that the wisdom and art had not been lost to them. Nor had the human design lost that skill. I was about to bear witness to the re-evolving and re-awakening of sacred dryad and human relationships. And the true power of the totem's reception and transmission. As an actual staff working on behalf of the whole spiritual essence of a land!

The totem rose from roots deep within the ground, its 'construction' like a bird's nest being built in fast forward. It rose past the central oak beam, onwards and up and up, continuing on through the original sleeping platform, emerging through the roof until it towered high above the cottage like a mystic aerial. And the materials of its form were vast and varied, with every type of leaf, twig and branch intertwined in an organically woven totem. Each facet radiating the signal that every tree spirit uniquely resonated with.

Like attracts like, I thought as I watched the miraculous assembly of this lofty signal post. Each frequency blend is specific to its particular species of tree. From towering oak, through abundant variance of flower, to every type of blade of grass, everyone has its own 'barcode'.

What stood before me was the most stunning organic sculpture, its features radiating with each unique frequency band. This was now a central hub created to bring in and temporarily house the hundreds of tree spirits from miles around. For just as undines, water spirits and sylphs, air spirits must travel within the material 'body' they are the life source of, so too must the dryads occupy the physical home they are the essence force of. Between the wisdom of the oak and its connective web to the miles of woods and countryside surroundings, and the delighted assistance of all the house spirits too, an energetic cobweb had been spun.

It was almost sensory overload as, from North, South, East and West, the elemental beings flooded in down these intricate threads. Akin to watching electricity travel down wires, I held fast to the connection as a veritable circus act played out before me.

'Zip wiring' to the centre, rejoicing in their reunion, as the cottage walls appeared to bulge with the sheer emanation from the force that arrived. The heady fragrances and freshness of the woodlands and pine forests permeated its entirety. Walls, floors, roof, every single cell, sucked in the bounty of its zest and purity. This was a cleansing and re-alignment on a grand scale.

With pure essence effervescence. As I delighted with them, deep down, I knew the lives held much harm and trauma within its own community. So great that it had seized this healing opportunity to unify around, teach and guide me like never before.

Pushing that aside for the moment, I continued to hold the focus. A miracle of elementals at work in harmony, the energy of the cottage was lifting, lightening, held in the vibrancy of teams of eager workers. An abundance of spruce and pine energy had purified the indigo and deep green force permeating so every corner looked sharp and clear.

Then, in the bedroom, a sleek cat appeared. Although a long passed resident, her powerfully attuned feline energy messaged to me that indeed the place had been lifted out of many lower frequencies. As I watched her numerous more cats appeared, however these behaved as a family and later it was confirmed the previous occupant had an abundance of cat companions. It was, however, the singular much earlier resident whose purrs trilled ever louder as the cleansing peaked. Satisfied, she rubbed herself against the totem clearly revelling in the atmosphere. As she stretched up happily clawing the 'pole'. I realized that in synchronicity with the whole orchestra of energies she was telling me, "I see this too. Yes, all of this is real. Every layer and life form is playing its part here today."

As if she was a gatekeeper to earlier times, my mind's eye found itself pulled to the adjoining house and garden. There a towering tree emitted palpable distress. Locked on magnetically to an ancient emanation of shock a cart lumbered into view. The three male occupants leapt off and began dragging a heavy weight from it. Healing force held me steady as I realized it was a severely beaten man whom they then began to hang by a rope from a tree that had occupied that very space prior. It was a callous and cold act and I felt deeply for the tree and the three men calling for redemption. For the man hanging wore the 'uniform' of a man of the cloth. Trees and land were scarred by the act and the Reverend I knew too was not at rest. The ground they buried him in was not hallowed ground and the unease from his soul saturated the earth all around.

I willed to pull away from that time and harm, but the collective consciousness of the trees held me with their need and mission. "What do I need to understand?" I transmitted. Immediately a Lych gate swam into view. Words that pricked shame in me echoed through. Every word penetrating. 'Lych gates. Hanging trees. Humans have used us in their atrocities and cruel acts. What of us who become Lych gates? Became the trees upon which lives were taken?'

'The public hanging tree where crowds gathered, soaking our roots with their fear and thirst for revenge? Stunting our growth, our evolvement with stains of their primitive actions and coarse emotions. Some of us have borne that pain ever since. All feel it with us. Innocent we are, yet made to be a part of the crimes.

'To carry the pain and suffering in our very beings for eternity. Unless you help those of us who call you now to change that print. You hear us. Heal us now please.'

My face ran with tears as pictures played through my mind. Suicides? Public hangings? Gallows? Giant jaws of destruction as monstrous machines clear cut a swathe of pine forest, toppling rows of trees like matchsticks. No sense of the life of nature, the balance and sensitivity of earth. Just a commodity to be used and abused. A row of crosses on the horizon. What deeper distress than to be a part of a crucifixion? The collective consciousness and soul memory of the trees shed its sorrow upon me. I prayed for its healing. For the rise of human consciousness to greater, to kinder levels. To rise to do better. To fulfil the promise of the human family. Our design. The human purpose. To learn and rise up and walk gently upon this earth. To once more stand proud with our elemental friends. Honouring them. Working together as one. I promised to work on and answer the call ever deeper.

Gradually the pictures, the trees realities subsided. My heart sat like a stone in my chest. Everything hurt. Every cell wept. 'Pick me up.' My hands reached eagerly for the little staff. The sheer exuberance of the elementals thrilled once again through its being. Bringing me back, I would not forget. Gradually I rebalanced, thanking the whole mind of the trees. They had let me into the darkest reaches of their collective soul print.

The healer's place is to know it and to hold it, correct towards remedy and new. To know it, but not dwell or think about it, unless the direction of travel is towards better. To face the light and turn away from darkness, for the answers reside within and with the light. As I regained hold of those crampons of sanity and safety, my feet found solid ground and my heart and mind connected, firm and strong together.

What had been caused through human agency must be remedied by it. Nature had to share the burden, bring it into human consciousness. The first small steps toward healing had been made. Much lay ahead to do.

Alongside my 'return' and recalibration, the force within the cottage began to wane and the 'power lines' fizzed and popped to stillness. Despite the far reaching needs the land energy healing had revealed, there was a greater levity that beamed like sunlight reflected off water. A gentle hum of wellbeing with a hint of new. Trees stretching their branches high and proud, their power and sensitivity now impressed upon the human soul and psyche.

For, once imbued within one, its truth now resides there for all to connect to. Hints of childlike overtones, as the elementals resettled, returning like children from a day of play together. Under the strong oak beam, I bade my goodbyes, promising a written report and to return, for much more called also within the house to do. It creaked and expanded, the soul of its being now carried too within me. No nature spirit had ever taught me so profoundly about the dignity and majesty of the trees.

As I left, my mind and systems swept the whole area like a radar. Reaching out to sweep every element and elemental into its thanks. Into its promise of continuance and return. Faithful pine twig still clasped in my hand I realized, 'Yes my staff does comfort me.'

Time now to make an equal return to nature. To each be a staff as we walk through the journey of our life. A beacon of respect. An amplifier of compassion. A transmitter of human dignity and true sensitivity. May Earth's soul yet be comforted by the human presence. Tomorrow beckoned. Another gift of a day. Another chance to try.

Chapter 15

Lost Souls

D onna was fixated upon the huge stone hearth. Caught in the dichotomy of feeling repelled but compelled, she backed away, then moved closer, her face pale, expression nauseous. She had been open to accompanying me to continue the cleansing of the cottage. And I had said little about the layers I had been shown on the previous visit. Always wiser to see what her acute sensing picked up on.

But that morning it had taken me on a confusing journey. Scrambling my inner sat nav, holding us at bay. Having driven directly there the first time, that line of direct attraction had been obscured by forces that made it clear it had no welcome mat out for us!

The approach of truth appeared by long hidden secrets. As the land had cleansed and risen in frequency its vulnerability to exposure was thus heightened. Just that short delay tactic had already informed us that the healing had a tough job lined up on its agenda today.

A sense of foreboding wrapped itself around me. Donna shivered and backed away farther. "I do not like that hearth, that fireplace. Whatever is radiating off that whole wall of stones feels bad, really bad here in the kitchen. And beyond grim in the bedroom. Sickeningly dark." I could only nod in agreement, all hopes that my radar had been off course on the previous cleanse now fully dashed. Today's work was not going to be a myriad of new experiences in nature's classroom with 'Teachers' eagerly awaiting their human students. That boundless generosity and loving sense of reconnection felt so distant now in the saturation of heavy coarse emotions all around.

In sync we both swung round to the left corner of the kitchen. It was a masculine presence from way back on the timelines. A heavy sense of a persistent someone the homeowners had regularly felt in that room. "He's not exactly radiating sunshine either," Donna mused. The general blend of misery, anger and sadness was trying hard to flatline us into its stum, so I turned my back on it, busying myself unpacking incense and chimes. At the bottom of the bag lay a variety of crystals and bottles of solarised gem waters which I fished out too. "For some reason these seemed to be needed today. Am not sure why?"

Donna barely acknowledged. She had squared her stance and had already immersed herself in reaching into the past and the origins of this man's dark presence. "He's a man of God," she declared, "a Priest. And he is reading from the Bible. Whatever happened here he knows. He cannot rest. The only way to help him is to work out what the heck has gone on here. He is angry. It's an abomination. A sin. That's what he says. That's what he believes."

I listened quietly. Independently the house and land had now taken us both to a scar involving an ordained life. If this was the same man whose life had been taken, had he been silenced because of discovering some crime that had occurred here? What had they done with his body? Where in the 'Lawless Land' had he been buried? But this felt more than a cry for his own soul lying in unconsecrated ground. Whatever had led him to this place to meet that untimely death, that ministry and mission within him still awaited its completion. An agitation in his soul memory that was spiking peaks in the very heart monitor of the old settlement. A fatal wound that was enabling alarm bells and distress signals to surface. Our senses were now on hyper alert, our full attention as honed as a critical care nurse. No time to confer. No way to un hear and desensitize. The 'patient' was on the table bleeding in front of us. Donna snapped back into the present as training, and a host of powerful healing essences moved into us. She pointed upwards. I agreed. The exposure of the truth lay in the bedroom above.

The rudimentary ladder leading to the sleeping platform above was vivid now. As the bedroom revealed its former rough bare beginnings a sooty blackness seemed to pulse through the wall. Tendrils of screaming fear and pain seeped up the chimney breast. Fire and flames had sought to purify, but had never quite been able to burn the presence of the evidence away. But of what? We steeled ourselves. Wiped our minds clear. And surrendered to that time and space.

Aching pain-soaked walls spilled and purged themselves. Breathtaking agony slammed into our guts. Two women, one frantically insistent on her work. The other lay on a dirty low platform, wailing, bleeding. We had seen enough. Now we knew. Air. Our lungs cried for air, our whole being for sunlight to bleach us clean, bathe us with pure light. Racing down the stairs, falling out the back door. Gulps of oxygen. We clung to each other and wept, as the beautiful pendulum of understanding rebalanced us, for so many need this healing to be won.

Abortion was messy, agonizing and so very dangerous then. Only a desperate woman would seek it out. Bear the agony of the rough crude methods and abject pain. Losing blood, baby and possibly her own life. If she survived, she did so to be seen as a sinner. Damned if she bore a child out of wedlock. Damned if she didn't. Ever more believing there was a black mark on her very soul. Unlikely ever again to be able to carry a child. Not from a womb savaged and battered. A barren womb that's further seen as God's punishment. If she survived the blood loss the later likely infection could carry her off instead. How many women died along with their unborn fetuses back then? How many survived, wrecked by shame?

And how many believed the infection a punishment and surrendered themselves to purgatory, locked in guilt? When you open a door to pain all who suffer it walk through. We cried with all who finally stepped over that threshold into the hands of pure love, understanding and forgiveness. A river of tears we willed and prayed one day soon will run dry.

Eventually the steady rise in our energy kicked in as we set out our minds clearly on the intent. Sorrow, however deep, must be clawed back from. It is the healer's job and call to service. It is what we asked for. Agreed to. Trained to fulfil. We grounded, located our intactness and centred squarely and equally into our mind and heart. And returned to the kitchen.

In the 'lawless land' it made sense that such 'services' could be located. A place where such 'help' to desperate women could be sought out. We silently observed space opening up to consider the women who had offered it. Yes, in the depths of darkness the drive for money alone can power the motive. But there was grave danger in providing abortions. How many who did so were compelled by compassion to help the most desperate of women? What bravery did it take to do so with the crudest of methods at their disposal?

The healing wrapped its understanding, love and forgiveness around them all. For those who had done this with pure heart and intent did so bravely. Believing they too would be judged for their actions. However turning away a fellow human soul wracked with desperation and facing judgment that would also rain down on the child all of its life added a weight to the other side of the scales. For what if the greater 'sin' was to not help? To turn the life away that perhaps some greater power of guidance had brought purposely to your door? In the moral maze there is no black and white, cut and dried answer. Each situation uniquely stands within its own merits and circumstances. And it is not WHAT we do, but WHY we do it that is either our saviour and sanctity, or our redress.

Emerging from that unified mind and heart space, we stood before the kitchen fireplace. "How many?" I asked. We counted together, both stopping at ten. Ten aborted fetuses committed to the flames of the fire. Donna's eyes closed, listening, hearing the Priest's call. "He needs to baptize and bless them all. Lift their souls to Heaven. He says to him they are locked in damnation but innocent. Once baptized they will be released and rise into God's hands where they belong."

Now I knew why the solarised pure gem waters were needed, but there was much to do to set the ecology correctly. It would be a great honour to facilitate this ceremony and our intent would be that it brought settlement and closure to all lives involved. Including the Priest.

I set out making charged water. Only those ordained, it is said, can create 'Holy Water'. However I had been caused to bring purified water, which had already been imbued with specific crystalline and colour frequencies, powered by the solar forces. With the addition of salt and healing forces transmitted into it, the water would change state. Pass from a liquid fluidity to a more 'plasticized' form, which when tipped would appear to move as one body that seemed almost congealed. We had an ordained presence anyway waiting to add the 'missing official connections.'

Holding fast to that fault line we watched as each Mother stepped forward. Bearing their babies and their souls one by one to the Priest to baptize. With each mark of the cross on their foreheads, his anguish calmed. Redemption bringing the release that washed guilt and sorrow away. And in that unified presence of a sacred ceremony we all prayed together. Until the sweet release of transition was finally won.

As the last tendrils of the basilica incense disinfected the walls, we closed the windows on that time. Sealed in the newfound settlements. Willed the best of memories to now emerge. Our awareness weighing heavy with the price the soul life of the land, trees, rocks still paid for the acts of human hands.

At numerous times ahead our attention was pulled back to the layers of distress in this land. The staff continued to connect me and reveal scenes of lives taken, suicides, murders and lives buried without markers or trace. Men, women and infants too poor, unloved or alone to receive anything other than a pauper's grave amidst the vast swathes of wild land.

On both visits, time over, I had been caused to stand for long periods only feet from the cottage's boundary, adjacent to the corner of the kitchen Donna and I had first seen the Priest appear in. Deep unease had acidified my stomach. Whatever I had done the bile never quelled. It still rose each time I wondered what became of the heavy bundle pulled from the cart. The remains of the Priest? A soul still disquieted by lying in unconsecrated ground?

One night a name impressed itself upon me repeatedly so I typed it into the search engine. Newspaper articles and potted historical accounts rolled up on the screen. It was the name given to a tree that had stood alone above those woodlands. Countless thieves, convicted criminals over many years, had been hung from this tree. A stark warning and deterrent for all to see. The original tree had long ago died, but in its place stood a now mature replacement planted in memory with a plaque laid inscribed with its name.

As I read on I realised suicides by hanging were still occurring in that place. The whole woodland was reaching out to shut that repetitive signal down. For Humans' sake and theirs...Enough. The first time I took one of the crystals with me that had been instrumental in the remote healing. After gathering an attunement to the closest family of trees around, all resounding with the layers of scars, I buried the crystal deep in the roots of the tree. Another moon cycle of transmissions passed before Donna and I returned together.

Each tree was touched, held and heard. The healing ran deep into their root structures, the interconnected webs of communication between them all carrying the balm and blessings of recovery to new for miles around. As I stared out over the panoramic view the tree commanded, I retrieved the little staff from my pocket, "You are home again now. Your work is done. May greater peace in your collective soul prevail."

And we left it to lie where it had tenderly been placed. Back in its familiar woodland home. Under the highest tree... for, of course, it was a beautiful Douglas Fir pine tree!

Chapter 16
Revelations of Reunion

Part 1

Dusk was beginning to throw its first shadows. That narrowing window between day and night caused the task of unloading and stacking the day's haul of wood to be hurried, carelessly noisy. Back and forth to the teetering pile of severed tree limbs. Adding, rebalancing. The pile adjusting itself precariously. Hollow clunks rang out, reverberating, trilling around the rusted tin walls of the old Anderson shelter.

Twice he stopped in his tracks. Fevered breath blending with the swirling grey tendrils pulsing around him. Just vapours from the labours of his task? Or was the atmosphere getting heavier, thicker with each load he dropped? Forcing himself back through the tunnel like darkness his shadow merged with the gloomy shapes cast by hay bales stacked high. A careless stumbling step entangled his right foot with the rusty innards of an old mangle. Arms akimbo, every muscle tightening, as the fight for balance ensued. Mere seconds caught inside the flailing battle to remain upright seemed to stretch bizarrely. A clumsy slow motion half dance, part fall, broken by the unyielding bulk of the hay. Tinder dry blades pierced his hands. Ran like needles through his clothes. Anguished yelps travelled through the dust clouds. The grey tendrils responding, merging into a darkly forming shape.

Dazed he resolutely wiped the pin pricks of blood from his hands and squared his sights on the wood saw by the now darkening semi-circle of light. Sores and wounds had to wait. Focus was paramount to operate the wood saw. Just enough firewood to fuel the kitchen hearth for tonight would do. His mind's eye stretched to the cozy sagging armchair that would soak up warmth luxuriously from the glowing orange embers.

Responsively his body had just begun to shake off the bone chilling ache the day's labour had caused, as fat wet rain drops first pitter pattered, then thundered down. Bouncing as they met the steely resistance of the old structure. Cold sweat forged a river down his spine as the wind whipped the corrugated sheets from their creaking responses to groaning, grating squeals.

Arms were laden heavy with the night's fuel as the first rod of lightning cracked and earthed. Blade of the saw was slicing, whining lethally through the first tree limb as thunder lent its Thor's hammer to the crescendo.

Splintering wood joined nature's chorus as the dark form enveloped him. Octopus like tendrils of anger, anguish permeated into every nerve ending. It wrapped itself around him like a shawl, rendering his arms useless. Swinging like pendulums by his quaking sides, halted in their task. A sense of wild desperation yanked his feet from their leaden state. "NO, NO, NO. NOT again", he wailed, his bewildered eyes taking in the form oozing the fury of its warning force. Too close, way too close to his face.

As its power connected with his fear, his senses located flight mode. Feet that had barely backed inches suddenly turned and broke into an adrenaline fuelled sprint. The accompanying screams pouring from panting, gaping mouth seeming to find a rhythm with his pounding steps. Fast jerky glances behind him confirmed there was no pursuit. Worn sturdy cottage door protested at the rough shove, rebounding it back into his face. Inside. Slam. Bolts, locks and chains forced, jimmied, propelled home.

He slid wearily down the door, breathless, scared, alone on the cold flagstone floor. The hearth stared mocking and cold. Empty again it would remain. The sturdiness of the old cottage walls brought some comfort as his heaving chest slowed. As the icy hard floor added its insult to his injuries, he slowly raised his arms and hauled himself to his feet. Shaking legs adjusted, recalibrated, carried him towards the old pantry. Thank goodness this was not now some primitive shelter and he was a woodcutter of times long past.

Flicking on the central heating and the kettle too, the young man picked up his mobile phone and hit the dial button. Audible relieved sighs escaped him as it was mercifully answered on the second ring. "Mum, you have to find someone now to help. And fast. I really, truly, know now this place is haunted."

My phone rang next.

Part 2

As the engine ticked and cooled, conflicting feelings ran numerous programs in each sense. Much of the small holding could be viewed from the position I had been pulled into and its very being was laying its soul bare instantly. The entirety of its land was drenched in sadness so raw it physically pained. Yet it was very clear this gloom hovered like a dense blanket, a top coat in a shade called 'despair' applied in very recent history. For below lay endless layers of warmth.

Bountiful emanations of welcome. A veritable burning fire of delights. Nowhere had ever won my heart so fast. Or intrigued and delighted me so completely. "Hello, you all," I whispered, "I am going to liberate you if it's the last thing on earth I do."

The muted elemental responses and barren stillness only heightened my resolve and sharpened senses further. In terms of 'show and tell' everything was doing its utmost to lay bare the hurts and harm in total clarity. Such open honesty was a very rich blessing to work with and for.

Brief introductions soon revealed that the young man had, from numerous 'strange' experiences in the Anderson shelter, now moved from abject skeptic to terrified believer. A few words to the wise to take the edge off that were duly swapped over coffee. A previous attempt by another healer had not made any impact on settling the disturbances and phenomena which particularly manifested most strongly when the electric saw was turned on. Being a tree surgeon it was a vital part of the kit so needed tasks were not being achieved. Not only had the presence impressed its upset and anger so strongly that it felt every hair on his head and body was standing to attention, but there was also the added evidence a camera he had installed had revealed.

A definite figure regularly flitting across its sight. I gently turned down the offer to view it. That this was a relatively young woman was already clear to me. And turning the camera off was necessary first.

By that time he had only been living there a few weeks. Having previously been delighted at being offered the 'perfect' place to rent, his fear was now ramped up to the point of wanting to cut and run. I had a keen sense that the landlord's rent was very low because his turnover of recent tenants was very high! Reassuring him that the very essence of the place was wonderful and that the phenomena would be explained and resolved, I set to work.

I needed all the daylight hours I would get to wrap up this first most important land healing because it was already clear that the life of the place would run on within me and bid me back for its own desires.

A dwelling had nestled into this landscape for centuries and its welcome sight had left the echoes of rejoicing hearts and the frivolities of companionship bursting to be freed from below the recent traumatic shock waves. There was a sense of great pride wrapped within a quiet modesty. A cleaving to its oath of protection that shone like a shield in the very aura of its presence. Humble had its origins and evolving forms been, but strong was its tenet of integrity.

The walls and land spoke their truth clearly. And because it loved so deeply, respected so fully and honoured protection in every cell of its whole, whoever was held here would be so until their needs were met. This pact whispered from every blade of grass. There would be no opening up and racing towards its own salvation and relief for the sake of itself. I would have to understand, recognise and respect at a resonance equal to its for it to release this life into mine and the healing's hands. Our greetings and agreements secured, my feet headed for the Anderson shelter. The air thickened as I passed from the semi-circle of light into its dim, dank interior.

Halfway through the structure, and feet stopped dead in their tracks. A wall of wretched fear and anguish hung so solidly before me, its force field swallowed me into its reality. The now scattered hay bales were stacked high within its form. A rope hung, swinging hypnotically from high above them. Head pounding, legs buckling, I doubled up at the sight of her, stacking the hay, mounting the pile, head through the noose, legs flailing, kicking the hay bales, tumbling. Acid seared bitter in my scorching throat, "Enough, enough," I called out, "I see. This much I understand."

The woman was wretched and thin, late 30s early 40s. A once bonny bright life ravaged by illness. She had taken charge of the ending of her life. But I knew too well how many suicides by hanging did not break the neck instantly. Instead the victim choked. A prolonged anguish.

But this was not just a trauma print. This woman had missed her window to pass over and something was holding her here. What was troubling her even more than her own awful demise? And why did she react so strongly and angrily to the noise? "Show me more," I implored gently. "You can trust me. I will help you. Tell me what you need me to understand." The impenetrable wall lifted and I followed as she led me out of the shelter onto the land.

Walking the wide open pasture land, time ticked by. The woman was gone from my vision, in a strata of time my systems would need to locate. Quiet inner conversations ran on, the land opening up with each circuit I took. Soon each ley line that crossed the land became familiar force fields to walk through and along. Layers of history swam through my vision. Sheep, a whole lot of sheep! Carts carrying strong men and women. Herding, working the land. Tier upon tier of past times imprinted solidly, held with joy. A rich endless tapestry of its own simple story. Of its being and life.

As machinery became more modern and carts were replaced by trailers and tractors, I saw in my peripheral vision a brilliant blue haze rising over the horizon. 'The river flows there.' Words crystal clear within me. Our communion had reached completion. 'Those are the Elementals of the Riverbank.' A drifting ethereal mass of part dragonfly and part butterfly shaped forms hovered above the river. Its brilliant forget me not blue hung like a delicate flower wall, each finite being distinct within the unified force it was of.

"Air elementals who are carriers of water," I was told further as I feasted on the spectacle and committed the mental pictures deep into my memory bank. "When your task is complete they will come and wash the land clean." I transmitted my thanks to the beautiful beings, sank deeper into the arms of the small holding and waited.

Before me the open pastureland morphed into a well hewn meadow. High fencing surrounded a large portion of it and within that compound grazed the three horses. The woman appeared, now as clear as if still embodied and in health. She entered the compound and with practised skill saddled a horse and swung herself up onto its back. Horse and rider became one. The pleasing aromas of horse, leather and grass emitting as she cantered around the paddock.

These were her passion and her devotion. Beautifully cared for. A reciprocal love. 'What do you need? Show me more,' I willed. She dismounted. Exited the paddock and walked back through the shelter heading for the cottage. I quickly followed. Her energy was magnetic, drawing on all my senses yet not draining them. Through the front door across the kitchen and into the small front lounge;

she strode over to the window and stared out over the meadow.

Standing by her side, my hand found hers and our tears fell as they joined.

"See over there?" she gestured to a large hook on the ceiling beam. "I understand," I replied. Deep pain ran through me at the reality of the lonely act of planning. Realizing the ceiling was just too low. "It was cancer. Terminal. Took my life from me. I would not let that own my death too. My terms on my time." I looked deep into her eyes. Brave. Strong. Our tears ran.

"So I had no choice but to do it in the shelter. How could I know it would take so long? And my distress frightened the horses. I hurt the most precious lives I have. So I could not go. I could not leave them. I have to protect them from any more harm and distress." "And the saw will frighten them," I said. "Of course. I understand. I knew you meant no harm." Tightly holding her hand I asked the guides where the horses had been taken. The relief was great that they were still all united. Taken by new owners but stabled together. Thank goodness for the intuition and kindness within those dear people to act so wisely. "They will take you to them now," I told her. "Take all the time you need to be with them and say your Goodbye's. When you return, the healing and the land will release you onwards."

Time passes differently when inside of its life and state. So how long went by I have no idea. The directive was to hold the connection and will the peace and restoration through her whole. Immersed in the horses' natural joy of sensing their loved one again, the healing flowed.

Embedding deep settlement into their beings. Negating the trauma and harm. It wrapped them tightly in the arms of forgiveness and assured them their next meeting lay only an ethereal breath away. And the land and cottage breathed in the healing with them. For it had loved them dearly and hurt from the sudden severing the physical ending had brought.

Ached for the time it too had been robbed. They had been happy together. And something in the pleasing notes of harmony in a relationship building with humans and animals together hinted at me of insights yet to come. There would be more wonders yet to behold!

I saw the replay of the day begin to run before she returned. Horses bucking and terrified, sirens wailing. The sounds of the helicopter blades of an air ambulance. A dedicated chaos of noise and attempts to save her, revive her. All well intentioned. But all adding to the confusion and distress. The scene died away as she returned. Already younger, lighter, free. A portal opened before her and I encouraged her through. "Step into the light, brave spirit. All is now well. Well done for your strength to guide me so well."

She smiled as her feet connected with the pathway into her new journey. As the portal shrunk and disappeared there was an audible upsurge in the pitch of the energy. Visual shifts within the land swam and morphed before my eyes. And a cloud of blue elementals rose as one body and moved in to baptize with the cleansing rebirth. Warmth began to seep through the old stone walls, dank and darkness ejected.

Light bounced in rays as the ground unfurled, stretched and rejoiced. Every cell of its being had been compacted and suppressed under the heavy weight of sadness. My systems joined with its celebrations, delighted to feel all return to their true state of grace.

Incense and chimes in hand I returned to the Anderson shelter. The pure notes rang longer and clearer as the residual dense force shifted and the Basilica disinfected the last remnants of pain and harm away. At last the old tin shelter creaked contentedly back into its former reality. It could once again serve its function well. And the wood saw would be free to run as long and noisily as it wished!

It is said that in the gentle flurry of a butterfly unfurling its wings, those atmospheric ripples travel and subtly change the vibrations of energy way across earth's land. As I once again walked the small holding it vibrated with the harmony of a well-tuned engine. Those endemic pure blue air and water elementals had restored the natural resonance to every inch of its being.

A veritable choral symphony of the finest silken wings gently and knowingly returning it to its tranquility.

My day's work was complete. And knowing soon that nature would respond with a huge cleansing downpour, I bade the young man farewell. Assuring him he could press on with his work that evening and all would be well. But I would be returning for the cottage's needs very soon. Having promised to explain it all and arrange, I dashed to the car. The storm clouds had already begun their work!

Part 3

Just a few weeks later I was again zipping along the country lanes eager to fulfill the cottage's needs further. The intensity of the healing transformation had caused a profound communion between us. Never had a building or land quite shared its rejoicing so powerfully. Its returning grace bringing insights, visual pictures and a timeline of information that stretched back through hundreds of years.

It had begun with the words, "I was a Drover's cottage you know?" A gleeful chorus that broke into a swell of elemental insights that ran on that first day until late into the night. I became a part of their world, their reality as they pulled me into the wefts and threads that their rich interconnected tapestry is. A silken web, each strand sensitized and responsive to the whole.

Drover's cottages dotted the length and breadth of the country, all providing valuable shelter and grazing for the lives who drove their flocks for hundreds of miles. Immense feats of travel across hills and valleys. A time when human senses connected deeply, and naturally navigated, the Drover's cottages were pure beacons of sanctuary along the way. A long time had passed since that elemental woven grid had activated and joined so consciously with human systems.

Their service was to guide, protect and nurture. A serene sense of familiarity and appreciation between humans, flocks and elemental realm. Tracks, pathways and routes etched as deeply into those shepherd's souls as into the land itself. A hard life, but one of such stillness and peaceful communion. Natural unification of all Earth's life forces and beings.

Just as ancient churches were built upon ley lines to power the religious messages, the Drover's cottages too followed Earth's magnetic flow. Shepherds and sheep wove their way along them, like Aborigines singing along the song lines. Rudimentary were the dwellings, shelter for man and flock together. But their understated modesty caused them to shine as brightly as any Cathedral or Temple. A perfect example of Mother Nature as Earth's great church. The dwellings and their surrounding land radiated more Essence connections than many an altar.

The flock and its charge, the congregation they stood proudly to serve and protect.

As those wise Elemental Elders welcomed me into their unified embrace, the true magic of nature honed all sensory systems. It was a gift of reciprocation that caused my gratitude and values to soar. Every free minute our human and elemental reunion deepened. All lives drinking thirstily from the fountain spring of true connection that soon bursts from a trickle to a gushing stream.

I arrived to an evocative blend of strong ancient force and fine effervescent presence and gratefully set my bare feet back onto the land. The Anderson shelter nestled and bulged with neatly stacked hewn logs. The electric saw had run day and night without interruption. Amidst our reunions and revelations though had come some very specific requests from the cottage itself. The many changes and additions to its form over countless years had left it crying out for an anchorage to its 'original' footprint and sense of self. And a dear previous resident also had to be freed.

The cottage was cleaving to him as much as he was holding on to it. I could so understand how settling a long-term resident would be to a shelter where previously, although regular in their return, the occupants were so temporary and transient. I had first seen Jack as the simple richness and abundant joy of the place unfurled on the timelines. Resplendent in blue overalls or faded old baggy denims clinging to braces, old Jack had bedded into the small holding for over 45 years. The dwelling had embraced him as a part of itself, so richly enhanced by the continual rhythm of a contented soul within its vibration. Neither had been able to let go of the other. But now the cottage was ready. And so too was Jack. The day's work beckoned and excitement trilled at what might lie ahead!

As my feet grounded and revelled in the power of the newly uplifted land the front door opened. The young man's welcome mirrored the changes in his surroundings. Fear and confusion now replaced by curiosity and the hint of a shy smile. He had endured no hair-raising chills or need since to flee, and the well-being in the land had washed the tiredness from his face. Having explained the lady's story very clearly in the intervening weeks, he had also quietly transmitted his apologies to her. For he too had been touched by her life's ending and courage. The greatest relief always came with the understanding that 'phenomena' is so often simply a sign that life wills to pass onwards, but first needs to be heard.

Thus, his curiosity peaked, and knowing that now the cottage's 'haunting' was impressing itself upon him, I began to run through the history shown to me, choosing the words carefully to capture the pictures it had painted, now etched in my mind. Once I arrived at the strata of time dear Jack inhabited, he too began to appreciate the virtue of his presence there still. Fears dissipated with the reality of the heartwarming delight in the very soul of the cottage for the precious gift of a permanent resident.

Year after year Jack had tended the land, planted his back garden with pride and flowers and toasted his toes by the cozy kitchen and lounge fires. With each passing season he sowed, nurtured and harvested his crops, plowing a furrow of love and devotion. A harmonic rhythm of nature and man in synch the land held with such easy familiarity, that when Jack died the contented flow simply ran on inside of its strong established currents. House and land contained his energy, simply protecting and sheltering his presence as an intrinsic part of itself. So, Jack had missed his window to pass onwards. And various changes to the cottage since had unsettled both considerably. I began to bring the 'historic account' to a speedier conclusion as man and dwelling became more insistent. Beckoning the present tenant to follow, I surrendered to their compulsion and headed out the kitchen as instructed.

First to the small hallway where, once again, complaints were raised about the repositioned staircase! But all the action and dissatisfaction lay just a few steps further on in the bathroom. Stepping over the threshold I halted abruptly.

The shower cubicle was to my right and then beyond a small extension housed the remainder of the suite. This part of the room did not even figure in the cottage's sense of itself, so had an empty soulless lack of any atmosphere. But it was the print by the shower cubicle which was incredibly strong. And my desire to walk through the smoothly plastered wall opposite it was overwhelming.

"You feel the presence most strongly here," I stated. He nodded, fear flickering again, "Every time I shower it's like someone is standing right there in the bathroom with me." Both keen to escape the confined space, we hurried out of the front door and circled round to the back of the house, where its old thick walls confirmed my compulsion and Jack's confusion!

"See that area of cleaner stones, well that was where the original back door was. That leads into a little porch where the shower now stands, so the door was directly opposite it. Also the stairs were not then a direct flight as they are now. They dog legged from the porch, and coats were hung under them. The natural flow of the energies are so strongly held in this place, so you are sensing the density of the prints of human traffic, in and out, and up and down. Now Jack is used to those well-worn tracks. And he is ready to leave. In fact he has been insisting you hear him and impressing himself upon you. All the cottage needs to do is release him. I am certain that when it shows him the door, then the last of its previous tenants who have found themselves Earth bound will be safely taken onwards. Just leave me here to open up that familiar route for him and then I must do some cleansing work inside."

With a relieved sigh and a firm shake of my hand he wandered off to his work. For such a quiet young man much passed in that gesture. His recent learning curve had been quite steep!

Within seconds I was tumbling down the rabbit hole, merging fully with the heart of the smallholding where dear old Jack was held so strongly. "I know it's hard to let go," I encouraged. The Ancient walls shimmered in and out of view. So often in this work physical forms bend and distort, then matter disappears as you merge with the reality that all is pure energy. The physical world of matter is such a tiny part of the actuality. A minute sequin inside of numerous vibrational states of being and forms. Awesome that energy can condense into matter. And special that Source can experience aspects of itself transmute into forms and shapes. That truth is seen in the miracle of ice crystals for as the water freezes it reveals each unique exquisite design. No snowflake ever being the same as another.

What splendour of vibrations of energy can produce a rose? But how can conscious knowing be confirmed and returned to Source without human senses to feed that information back?

When we smell the perfumed scent of a rose, for whom and what do we breathe in its aroma? If our intention is so set, we, through the miracle of our human design, are proving the existence of creation unto itself and enabling it to witness what it actually looks like in physical form. As I merged ever deeper with the vibrations of the land I wondered how far and wide the source could sense the many beautiful facets of itself.

Riding the streams of its life force, the old door swam back into view. Jack donned his Wellingtons in the familiar confines of the old porch and lifted his coat from the hook for the last time. He strode smiling and waving, out into the back garden. Neat and colourful, it delighted the senses and, as I savoured the pride his dwelling held in his heart, I realized the doorway itself had acted as his portal into the next phase of his journey. For across the fields beyond stood his wife and son, their bright ginger hair complimenting the lush green grass of the field. Dear Jack had lived alone for many years. As their smiles radiated, and the warmth and power of reunion surged, I stepped out of their space and returned inside. The cottage was calling me upstairs.

Throughout the next hour or two my systems, senses and I time travelled with the small holding. From its inception as a rudimentary shelter where sheep, hens and humans all huddled together, to its more refined structure with a loft-like floor above. Where cleaner hay to sleep upon afforded 5-star accommodation and a good vantage point to keep an eye on the precious livestock too.

Further along it became a small Farmstead and, although still basic, the luxuries of a wooden bed appeared with more defined living and cooking spaces below. The livestock were now housed inside in shelters of their own.

As the 'film' played and the time lines rolled past, lesser energy in the memory prints were soothed, as though the healing ran like a hot press smoothing out kinks and creases. Eventually a high whistling note of pure force rang throughout against a background hum of content tranquility. In return for its centuries of service the healing essences and elementals had made their return in a profoundly special way. It was as though loyalty, honour, unity and protection along with many more fine values and principles had themselves, at core, been polished and now shone in their full splendour and radiance. One land healing had travelled the interconnected threads, high, far and wide.

Something stirred from deep within me. A desire to merge with nature, with Earth, like never before. The question rose before it was conscious. "Could I ask you, cottage and land, to show me what it feels like to be you? What is your sense of being and belonging as a part of earth herself?" The response was immediate. "Of course. Sit down on the floor."

Kneeling down I relaxed and waited. Gently my whole upper body rocked forward. A beat passed and then it slowly rocked back. Another 2 beats, then forwards again. On and on it ran. The tick tock of the same pattern and rhythm. Swaying naturally to the very heart beat that pulsed throughout that special place. Every structure, blade of grass, flora and fauna lived with that pulse, moved to that beat. In my mind's eye the blue elementals rose again above the river, circling, joining the sacred unified dance. "The river is tidal," they chorused. Of course! I was a part of the ebb and flow, the tidal force which all swayed in harmony with. No individual identity. A living reality of all only knowing itself as a part of the whole.

I stayed kneeling, immersed in the all-encompassing rhythm of Earth's heartbeat. Its power and presence indeed was immense. No wonder Jack had been held so strongly inside of its currents. The magical flow permeated every cell until I could not imagine how I had never felt the force of this pulse before. Until there, inside and with Earth's consciousness, with the arms of the Universe wrapped tightly around me, I realized at age 46 I had all along been finding what I wanted to be. All I had needed to do was unlock who I was born to be.

In prayer I bowed, kissed the ground. Blessed the place that had guided me home. Tender as ever to one of its flock. I stretched, stood tall, knowing I had finally grown up! Found the rich simplicity of what I was intended to be. Proved to be a warrior. To live. To grow. To try.

My footprints stared back at me, clearly etched in the dust of the floor. A symbolic trail of pathways taken, experiences passed and those still to come. Placing my feet delicately inside of each distinct print, I walked the rich tapestry of my own life, wending out of the cottage into the blissful sunlight. So many threads to be revealed. So many more words to stitch together into chapters still... in time ahead...to be discovered in the pages of another book.

THE END

Author Biography

S ue Oosterwoud became an avid campaigner in the late 1980's whilst running a catering business with her chef husband Taeke. Active in movements for human rights and raising awareness about the environment, those passions caused an awakening which led her to pursue the bigger questions of life.

Having always been aware of an instinctive and intuitive flow and communion that accompanied her from a small child, she was led by the quest to meet like-minded people and set her feet on a pathway of personal development in numerous ways. As life challenged and brought incredible happenings organically to her journey, sensitivity and awareness increased until the reality arrived that her life pursuit was to be a Healer. After 16 years of 'inner training' she placed her feet fully upon that pathway and a whole new world of communion and work for the worlds of energy burst forth!

Amidst establishing 3 therapy centres over many years and the healing touching innumerable lives, the medium of both Colour Therapy and Aura Cleansing created a harmonic attunement to sensing and creating ecologies. Alongside work in a school and university, there came an ever-growing call for healing to land and buildings, which heralded the most astonishing new learning and built the most intimate of relationships with the Planetary Elemental Kingdom.

Her life journey has held extraordinary experiences and a deep trusting relationship built with the worlds of energy. This book is about many of the pathways to that abundance and the healing work and mission it naturally created. It is as much their story, as her story, honouring the intention always to find truth and understand deeper the profound mysteries of the human design and the sacred planet we have been gifted to caretake and work for.

Sue now lives on the beautiful West Coast of Scotland, communing with the energies and capturing in words the journey since the last chapter of this book. The most testing of all yet travelled and also interspersed with many more experiences that happened during the life pathways this first book travels.

May this book bring hope, laughter and open up your world.

Blessings and Go Gently One and All

Thanks and Acknowledgments

There has been the great fortune of many teachers in my life thus far. Of those, the plethora of clients through whom I am indebted to learning the most. I ever hold thanks for their trust, their openness and the joys they bought in their new horizons. Nothing replaces real practical life learning and the charge of holding another's sacred worth and being in your hands and heart.

I would never have walked this journey, or known how to, without the invaluable wisdom and work within The Template Network. The cleanliness and purity of what they contain and caretake shepherded me and enabled me to train my own faculties and conscience in a way I have never met in any other network. I particularly thank Claire for her adherence and passion for the Well Being Sciences. There is no other pathway that would have enabled me to become the healer I have been allowed to be. Bless you for holding it with dignity and pride.

There has been no steadier or wiser hand on my tiller than Janet Roome, a blessed Reiki Master and Teacher to many. Thank you for always having just what was needed at the right time. Your generosity, nature and attunement is beautiful and always will be held in respect and love.

To my longstanding Spiritual Sister Nina Dauban, who gifted me my first 'break' into building the healing service, thank you for seeing the promise I was upholding in me. I trust you are proud of us. We have done well and still run with purpose intact and with joy! You have been my deepest companion in serving the Universe, deepening our human relationship with the Soul Lives of Mother Earth and driving always for the higher and finer in process and application. And held my hand and heart through the hardest times in my life. This book would not have been completed without your constant encouragement and practical willing assistance. I am blessed to know you on many levels! Thank you too to Nick for your typing assistance, your time and energy is hugely appreciated. Spiritual Warriors we are and will continue to be.

Many of the deepest and profound moments, and thus memories, happened because of the magical joining the Healing caused with Donna Austerberry. This book is, on numerous roads on the map, as much your journey as mine. It was a great joining of minds, hearts and intentions during our healing work together and we worked well! I am glad our friendship continues and it is a grace that we experienced and learned so much together in such profound ways. You will always be held in love and great thanks for who you are and your immense capacity for life.

And to Lynne McDermott, Crystal Angel and ever companion on every step of the journey too. Shine and Triumph! Your love is astonishing, as is your professional and intuitive sense of the human mind and heart. Thank you for helping mine through so much and to know itself better. You are a gift to the Planet and the Crystalline Worlds.

Part of the deepest of love I have experienced is held for my daughter Saskia, without whom I would never have learned the art of patience, or been so driven to quest quite so avidly to be the best version of human I can become at every step. You are beautiful inside and out, a superb Mum and a stunning Teacher. Your striving for excellence and passion for young people's lives and futures will endure within them always. You are the personification of the anagram of Teacher.... 'The Care'. Thank you for choosing me as your Mum. I guess you love a good project and us left of field characters! The rest of that deepest love is, and always will be, held for Taeke, your Dad. Master Chocolate Sculptor and Chef Extraordinaire, but most of all an amazing, bright, talented, enthusiastic and loving Husband, Dad and Opa. I know how proud he is of you. Blessed is the Communion and Connection we built which continues and evolves and always will do. Until we meet again, you are my Soul Mate and no one could have supported my life story like you and still does. I will continue to miss you with us all every day until then.

Lastly, but most importantly, to You All, Nature Spirits of Earth, Air, Water and Fire, your Realms are beautiful and incredible and your adhesion to purpose is astonishing. I will you are greater considered, far wider and deeper understood by all human lives and hope something of your greatness and worth is passed within these pages to raise consciousness and considered care for Earth and her soul lives one and all. Blessed I am with your kinship and the guidance and stewarding of the many Guardians, Guides, Angels and Essence Presences who have worked with and through me and attended. I am ever aware and conscious of your help and steering hands and voices. May our laughter, brevity and joy increase together and may

Earth rise to her promise as she is intended to be. For nothing has ever been so hard won and earned. Mother Earth, we are here and working for you.

Thank you to the small voice that became loud and awoke me. That quiet presence that I had always spoken with and companioned me. If you wish to discover who that is.....the next book will reveal.

Blessings. XXXX

Milton Keynes UK
Ingram Content Group UK Ltd.
UKHW050954190724
445790UK00008B/103

9 781835 381861